Cambridge Elements ≡

Elements in Publishing and Book Culture
edited by
Samantha Rayner
University College London
Leah Tether
University of Bristol

FANTASIES OF THE BOOKSTORE

Eben J. Muse
Bangor University

CAMBRIDGE
UNIVERSITY PRESS

CAMBRIDGE
UNIVERSITY PRESS

University Printing House, Cambridge CB2 8BS, United Kingdom

One Liberty Plaza, 20th Floor, New York, NY 10006, USA

477 Williamstown Road, Port Melbourne, VIC 3207, Australia

314–321, 3rd Floor, Plot 3, Splendor Forum, Jasola District Centre,
New Delhi – 110025, India

103 Penang Road, #05–06/07, Visioncrest Commercial, Singapore 238467

Cambridge University Press is part of the University of Cambridge.

It furthers the University's mission by disseminating knowledge in the pursuit of
education, learning, and research at the highest international levels of excellence.

www.cambridge.org
Information on this title: www.cambridge.org/9781108445399
DOI: 10.1017/9781108646000

First published 2022

A catalogue record for this publication is available from the British Library.

ISBN 978-1-108-44539-9 Paperback
ISSN 2514-8524 (online)
ISSN 2514-8516 (print)

Additional resources for this publication at www.cambridge.org/museappendix

Fantasies of the Bookstore

Elements in Publishing and Book Culture

DOI: 10.1017/9781108646000

First published online: June 2022

Eben J. Muse

Bangor University

Author for correspondence: Eben J. Muse, e.muse@bangor.ac.uk

ABSTRACT: This Element surveys the place of the bookstore in the creative imagination (the fantasies of the bookstore) through a study of novels in which bookstores play a prominent role in the setting or plot. Nearly 500 'bookstore novels' published since 1917 have been identified. The study borrows the concept of 'meaningful locations' from the field of human geography to assess fictional bookstores as narrative events rather than static backgrounds. As a meaningful location, the bookstore creates the potential for events that can occur both within the place of the store and in the wider space within which it functions. Elements of the narrative space include its spatio-temporal location, its locale or composition and the events that these elements generate to define the bookstore's sense of place.

This Element also has a video abstract: www.cambridge.org/museabstract

KEYWORDS: bookstore, narrative space, meaningful location, bibliomystery, bookselling

ISBNs: 9781108445399 (PB), 9781108646000 (OC)

ISSNs: 2514-8524 (online), 2514-8516 (print)

Contents

A further online Appendix: Bibliography of Bookstore Novels can be accessed at: www.cambridge.org/museappendix

Introduction: Bookstores in Fiction

The place of the bookstore in the creative imagination (the fantasies of the bookstore) through a study of novels in which bookstores play a prominent role in the setting or plot is the subject of this Element. A bibliography of more than 490 novels was compiled through a series of online searches of catalogues and social media lists. The Amazon.com catalogue was searched for the terms 'bookstore' and 'bookshop'. A similar search was conducted through the second-hand book catalogues of AbeBooks and Alibris, which added books that are now out of print. An additional search was conducted of the Goodreads' social media list 'Books about Bookstores', which included more than 280 titles. Blurbs, reviews and content from the books in these lists were investigated to separate fiction from non-fiction titles and to identify the role of the bookstore in the fictional works. The results of these searches were further developed through searches of book discussion sites, literary journals, bookseller catalogues and blogs. A total of 501 novels available in English (including eighteen in translation) published since 1917 were identified as what might be termed 'bookstore novels'. The complete bibliography is available online at https://bit.ly/book store_novel. Independent, used, antiquarian, second-hand, new and specialist bookstores have not been differentiated in the bibliography. Subcategories from the bibliography are provided in the online Appendix to the Element (Bibliography of Bookstore Novels) broken down into individual categories of fiction.

The bibliography, although extensive, cannot be described as definitive. In addition, the choice for inclusion or exclusion was sometimes necessarily subjective. Not every novel that included a bookstore in the narrative was included in the bibliography. The bookstore needed to be judged to play a prominent role in either the setting or the plot. Although a bookstore does appear in *Oliver Twist* (and its appearance is referred to in Section 1), for example, it would be misleading to refer to Dickens' novel as a 'bookstore novel'. Additional novels were added to the bibliography during the writing of this Element and it is hoped that the online bibliography will continue to be developed by other contributors. Further work in non-fiction books that are centred around bookstores is needed but that is outside the scope of this Element.

Murder and crime stories account for more than two-thirds of the bookstore novels identified. Murder among the shelves has been a popular theme at least since booksellers started dying in The Whisper on the Stair (Mearson 1924). The modern bibliomystery series, usually featuring a bookseller or bookstore owner who regularly becomes involved in murder, began when Lawrence Block introduced the bookseller-cum-burglar, Bernie Rhodenbarr, in his 1977 *Burglars Can't Be Choosers*. Since then, more than 300 books have been published in forty-seven individual series, most recently with Beth Wiseman's *The Bookseller's Promise* (2022). The longest running of these series, Caroline G. Hart's Death on Demand mysteries, produced twenty-seven volumes over the period of thirty years from 1987–2017. (A listing of these series in chronological order is available in the Appendix to this Element.)

Many of the bibliomystery series are self-described as 'cosy mysteries', a subgenre that typically includes romantic interests. Another seventy of the bookstore novels may be categorized as 'romance fiction'. Eighteen of the novels are categorized as LGBTQ+ or 'gay fiction'. These include the seven volumes of Josh Lanyon's *Adrian English Mysteries*, as well as Seana Kelly's two fantasy novels featuring Sam Quinn, a werewolf who runs a bookstore that caters for the supernatural community. In total, more than fifty novels of the fantastic were identified (including seven fantasy series) as well as fifty-five children's or young adults' novels.

The earliest novels in the bibliography are Christopher Morley's 1917 *Parnassus on Wheels* and its 1918 sequel, *The Haunted Bookshop*. However, the bookstore novel is mostly a twenty-first-century phenomenon. Only eighty-four of the books discussed in this Element appeared before 2000. In contrast, during the slightly more than two decades of the twenty-first century, starting with instalments in three separate mystery series (*Death on Demand*, *Dido Hoare* and *Honey Huckleberry*), more than 400 novels have appeared.

The increase in the bookstore novel since 2000 correlates with changes within the publishing industry itself. As Laura Miller has noted in her study of bookselling, *Reluctant Capitalists*, although the American Booksellers

Association (ABA) had historically included chains and independents, it noted a split in the needs and identities of these two retail groups in the 1980s and 1990s. In 1999, it shifted its membership to include only independents and started the Book Sense marketing campaign to support independent bookstores (Miller 2006, 183–4). In 2008, Book Sense was rebranded as IndieBound. A search using the Google Books Ngram Viewer for combinations of indie, independent, bookstore and bookshop shows no results for 'indie bookstore' or 'indie bookshop' before 2000. The first use of 'indie bookstore' is in *Alt.culture: An A-Z Guide to 90s America* in an article referring to 'indie bookstore bestsellers' (Daly and Wice 1995, 167). The number rises gradually until 2008, the year that the IndieBound marketing campaign began, totalling approximately sixty results. In the following ten years that triples to more than 270 resources using the term 'indie' to describe a bookstore or bookshop, suggesting the term 'indie' has gained in popular use. Given this context, it is worth noting that all the novels identified in the bibliography are set in independently operated bookstores rather than big box chains.

Throughout this Element, as reflected in the title, I have chosen to use the term book*store* rather than book*shop*. The former term dominates in the American media, while the latter is more common in the United Kingdom. The *Oxford English Dictionary* defines 'bookstore' as 'a bookshop' and 'bookshop' as 'a shop where books are sold' and Merriam-Webster offers the inverse. While one term emphasizes the collection (store) of books, the other stresses the commercial sale, reflecting perhaps the nature of these places as what Osborne described as a 'counter-space', 'revising the imperatives of commercial exchange supposedly defining the bookshop' (Osborne 2015, 143). The choice of 'bookstore' as the standard term throughout this Element, therefore, reflects my origins in America, but also my inclination toward the fantasy of these places as stores of books that are for sale.

This Element concentrates on novels available in English. Creative responses in other languages are only represented by the limited number of translated books. Films and short fiction have been introduced briefly for a wider context, but the examples provided are only indicative of a broad range of material to be explored. The International Movie DataBase includes more than 100 films that have 'bookstore' or 'bookshop' in the plot summary, starting with the 1916 silent film *Man and His Angel* (King et al. 1916). Gibbs Smith's *Art of the Bookstore* (Smith 2009) is an example of the visual responses. Although few video games to date have made use of bookstores, there is no reason to think the fantasy of the bookstore will not inspire them in the future.

The literature of bookstores extends beyond the novel. John Dunton's 1705 memoir, *The Life and Errors of John Dunton, Citizen of London With the Lives and Characters of More Than a Thousand Contemporary Divines and Other Persons of Literary Eminence* (Dunton 1818), may have been the first bookseller memoir to be published in English; it has been followed by a growing number of booksellers eager to share their experiences with books and book collectors. Carol Ann Duffy (Duffy 2016) and others have celebrated the bookstore in poetry. Bookstore tourism has spawned a genre of travel writing appearing frequently in many newspapers and magazines. The threat of bookstore closures brought on by the failure of Borders and the rise of Amazon created its own journalistic responses. Biographies, histories, recollections of bookstores and guides to the proper operation of bookstores – written by browsers, collectors, book-sellers, academics and novelists – provide a rich source for study beyond the scope of the current work.

1 The Bookstore as Meaningful Location

In *Oliver Twist*, Charles Dickens introduced the respectable Mr Brownlow being robbed at a bookstore, using the store as a border-space between the criminal world of Sikes and Fagin and the respectable world Brownlow inhabits. In the film version of Raymond Chandler's *The Big Sleep* (Hawks 1946), Philip Marlow visits two bookstores Geiger's Rare Books and the ACME Bookshop, identifying a similar border. Geiger's store is an obvious front for a pornography ring; the ACME Bookshop is a respectable-appearing store that closes suddenly for a romantic moment between the detective and the bookseller. As Paroma Chatterjee has pointed out, it is in the ACME Bookshop 'that we find the very heart of the twisted universe inhabited by the Sternwoods, Geigers, Marses and Marlowes' (Chatterjee 2020).

The bookstore is, by its very nature, a site of contrasts, providing a liminal space between commerce and culture, but also one between respectability and experience. Marlow's erotic adventures contrast sharply with Geiger's antiquarian respectability and ACME's intellectual clarity. But the used book trade in the 1930s did not often live up to these models. Jack Biblio and Jack Tannen, booksellers at Biblio & Tannen on New York's Book Row in the 1930s through 1950s, describe the space between culture and law that bookstores straddled:

> In the late 1920s and 1930s nearly all used bookshops in New York and in other cities around the country relied for at least part of their income on the sale of erotica – or, more accurately, pornography, since the sale of such material was outlawed and the laws were often vigorously enforced. This was before the landmark challenges to such censorship had gone through the courts and many booksellers found it necessary to risk handling the material under the counter in order to survive. (Chernofsky 1986, 1668)

The bookstore is a retail establishment that deals in packaged ideas. The value that it provides customers may be the ideas, the packaging or the space that contains the multiplicity of ideas. It provides the creative writer with what human geographers term a 'meaningful location' (Casey 1996; Cresswell 2009; Malpas 2018): a place defined by the possibility of unexpected and unplanned connections. As such, it is a mutable resource for creative writers. The potential of the store depends on its location, its layout and the books that it gathers. It is a collision point for numerous vectors: social, cultural, commercial, legal, respectable and dangerous.

A bookstore is also a physical place, as described by Lewis Buzbee in his memoir, *The Yellow-Lighted Bookshop*: 'A bookseller is, first and last, the custodian of a wonderful space, a groundskeeper concerned with the order and care and stock of that space. . . . Day-to-day bookselling is more about the physical world than the loftier realms' (Buzbee 2008, 107). As a physical place, the bookstore exists (even in a fictional existence) within what Jeff Malpas describes as 'a particular region of physical space or a location within it'. Malpas quickly expands that definition of space beyond its Cartesian limits, adding that place is also 'the frame within which experience (along with conceptions of self-identity) is to be understood' (Malpas 2018, 13). In other words, 'place' can be understood as a 'meaningful location', a space with an identity that persists and shifts within a spatio-temporal context. The relationships within the physical space (made possible by that physical space and happening across time) create a meaning that defines the place.

Doreen Massey describes of these relationships as creating 'chance of space':

> Space entails the unexpected. The specifically spatial within time-space is produced by that – sometimes happenstance, sometimes not – arrangement-in-relation-to-each-other that is the result of there being a multiplicity of trajectories. In spatial configurations, otherwise unconnected narratives may be brought into contact, or previously connected ones may be wrenched apart. There is always an element of 'chaos'. This is the chance of space; the accidental neighbour is one figure for it. (Massey 2005, 111)

John Agnew defined a 'meaningful location' as a space that provided a sense of place, 'the personal and emotional attachment people have to a place' (Cresswell 2004, 14). Cresswell expanded on the concept, defining place as a combination of location, locale and sense of place:

Location refers to an absolute point in space with a specific set of coordinates and measurable distances from other locations. Location refers to the 'where' of place. Locale refers to the material setting for social relations – the way a place looks. Locale includes the buildings, streets, parks, and other visible and tangible aspects of a place. Sense of place refers to the more nebulous meanings associated with a place: the feelings and emotions a place evokes. (Cresswell 2009, 1)

The use of the store as a 'meaningful location' will be considered in each of these texts. The fictional bookstores will be considered in terms of their locations, locales and the sense of place they create.

Location

As Cresswell makes clear, place is grounded in space, a geographical location where the place can be found. On its surface, this would appear to be the simplest aspect of place: its geographical coordinates, the intersection of its longitude and latitude, the GPS position, its what3words indicator. However, location also implies a relationship to other things, other places. A bookstore located at 41.70°, -70.24° is north of 40.69° and south of 42.71°. A store located at 222 Old Kings Highway may be expected to sit between numbers 221 and 223. Providing directions to a location, we typically use other landmarks: we might say 'it is just across the street from the restaurant' (Passini 1996; Hund, Schmettow and Noordzij 2012). A bookstore across the street from a restaurant is likely to differ in its sense of place from one on an isolated rural road. The former might attract diners who walk over while waiting for a table while the latter may require signage to attract people passing by in their car.

Location is not limited to spatiality. A place is also located in time. A mobile bookstore may be in a village square on Monday, a beach parking lot on Tuesday. The location, and its relationships to the other places, shifts each day. Likewise, a bookstore located near the ocean has a different set of relationships during the summer from the winter or during a hurricane or economic downturn. Staff in the store change from year to year (if not more frequently). The new store on the block may become an established business over the years and its owners may marry, divorce, have children or choose not to, suffer hardships, become bankrupt or simply age over time. Each visit to the store (fictional or not) becomes a snapshot of that specific time and place.

Locale

Events are made possible by the locale in which they occur, 'the material setting for social relations'. If a store stocks only English-language books, a non-English speaker will be limited to the covers, recognizing the names of authors or admiring the book designs. If a bookseller places a dollar-book table by the front door, they create the potential for people to gather there and hunt for bargains. They also define what the browser can expect on the other side of that door. Rules and conventions are also part of the locale, as are the customers who gather in the shop. A store that specializes in rare and antiquarian volumes may create an elitist setting, while a children's store is likely to be colourful and friendly.

The locale of the place gathers people, objects, histories, rules, languages, thoughts and conventions at a location, creating the possibility of action, interaction, movement, exchange (Casey 1996). The place thus becomes 'more an *event* than a *thing*':

> Rather than being one definite sort of thing – for example, physical, spiritual, cultural, social – a given place takes on the qualities of its occupants, reflecting these qualities in its own constitution and description and expressing them in its occurrence as an event: places not only are, they happen. (And it is because they happen that they lend themselves so well to narration, whether as history or as story.) (Casey 1996, 27)

Sense of Place

De Certeau describes space as 'practised place' (De Certeau 1984, 117) – a space becomes a meaningful location when practised. If a bookstore is understood to be a meaningful location, that meaning must be created through the dynamic play of the potential provided by its location and its locale by those who interact with or in that location. Game design theory is concerned with the creation of virtual but meaningful locations with which players can interact and its Mechanics-Dynamics-Aesthetics model is a useful tool for understanding the physical creation of meaning locations. Location and locale are the rules (mechanics) of a game world. They create the potential dynamics of the experience within that space. When an actor (a player in the game, but one of many possible roles in a bookstore – owner, browser, buyer, seller, author, staff) engages with the space, they bring their own contexts and preconceptions to the space. The interactions realize the potential of the location in an aesthetic experience (Hunicke, LeBlanc and Zubek 2004; Sicart 2008; Walk, Görlich and Barrett 2017). This Element refers to that experience, as it is expressed in the bookstore novels collected here, as the 'fantasy of the bookstore'.

Huw Osborne, in his study of *The Rise of the Modernist Bookshop*, describing the progressive bookstore in particular, notes that the bookstore gathers together both the commercial and the cultural into a single space. He describes the result as 'spaces that hijack dominant spaces and repurpose them to leisure or liberating ones. In doing so they question or change the nature of that dominant space'. He describes the bookshop as 'a counter-space, revising the imperatives of commercial exchange supposedly defining the bookshop' (Osborne 2015, 142–3). The confluence of culture with commerce means every bookshop is a disruption of both sides of the counter.

In her study of feminist bookstores, Kathrine Liddle identifies a model for a type of bookstore locale as 'cultural interaction spaces'. In a feminist bookstore, according to Liddle, the confluence of ideas, booksellers and audience means that booksellers and other customers are 'likely to share certain attitudes and ideologies that may have been less prevalent in mainstream venues'. While Liddle does not refer directly to meaningful locations as a concept, she does identify elements that echo Cresswell's triad of location, locale and sense of place. For Liddle, the elements are specific to bookstores and include staff and booksellers; books (the cultural products); physical space (its layout, design, visual attributes); atmosphere (language, behaviours, attitudes, inclusivity or exclusivity); interactions; customers and audience (Liddle 2019).

These elements combine to create an identity for the store and the potential for a community with common interests. It is this active combining, a constant gathering together that causes the intersection of vectors (lives, ideas, movements), that allows for particular actions. One example is Oldenburg's 'third place' (the other two being home and work), accessible spaces that 'serve to level their guests to a condition of social equality' (Oldenburg 1989). The space of the bookstore, in its various permutations of location, locale and sense of place, encourages communities around such common interest as LGBTQ+ rights, Marxism, Christianity, Black Lives Matter, Judaism, Arabic studies, Spanish-language writing and science fiction to name only a few of the types of specialist bookstore that exist.

The dynamic nature of a bookstore as a place that is an event, the many vectors that intersect by chance or design within any bookstore, create the potential for complex fantasies of the bookstore. This Element will apply the idea of a bookstore as a meaningful location to the bookstore novel. It will explore the sort of event the bookstore location has been for writers. An examination of the fictional bookstore as location and as locale will set the scene, followed by an examination of how the event plays out to create senses of place, in particular, the somewhat contradictory senses of the bookstore as a place of murder and mystery or as a place of safety and haven.

2 Location and Locale

Tales from Two Cities

New York and London were the centres of the antiquarian book trade at the start of the twentieth century. The London trade had been well established for centuries, with many of the major collections based there (Roberts 1895; Slater 1898). New York had been catching up and by 1900 had established its own antiquarian culture and trade. The auction in 1911 of the Robert Hoe Library, in which the American railroad magnate Henry E. Huntington bid $50,000 for a Gutenberg Bible – the highest price of any book up for auction to that date – established New York as the new premier centre for antiquarian book collecting. As the *New York Times* reported after the event: 'The London dealers, though they were active bidders, did not obtain many of the day's prizes' (TimesMachine 1911, 3). The famous London firm of Bernard Quaritch dropped out of the Gutenberg bidding after $30,000; only the two American firms continued the bidding after that. The story was a front-page sensation (TimesMachine 1911).

The bookstore in novels of the first decades of the twentieth century provided a similar contrast in fortunes. While the tone in American novels is optimistic (even in the face of murders and war), the British tales are decidedly less so. Two of the earliest fictions from America, Christopher Morley's *Parnassus on Wheels* (1917) and its sequel *The Haunted Bookshop* (1919) offer optimistic visions of bookselling and of literature's power to improve society. When the representative of an advertising company comes to his store, the proprietor, Roger Mifflin, tells him a bookstore has no more need to advertise than does a doctor:

> People don't know they want books. I can see just by looking at you that your mind is ill for lack of books but you are blissfully unaware of it! People don't go to a bookseller until some serious mental accident or disease makes them aware of their danger. Then they come here.
>
> (Morley 1923, 9)

Morley's two novels, written as the world faced its first world war, are paeons to the glory of the book and the bookseller. Roger Mifflin's passion for books overflows and inspires Helen McGill, a customer in a farmhouse he visits in the backwoods of New England, to leave her home and responsibilities to join the life of an itinerant bookseller. By the time of the sequel, the two are living in comfort upstairs from their New York bookstore:

> This bookshop, which does business under the unusual name 'Parnassus at Home,' is housed in one of the comfortable old brown-stone dwellings which have been the joy of several generations of plumbers and cockroaches. The owner of the business has been at pains to remodel the house to make it a more suitable shrine for his trade, which deals entirely in second-hand volumes. There is no second-hand bookshop in the world more worthy of respect. (Morley 1923, 1)

The London bookstore in Arnold Bennett's *Riceyman Steps* (1923) stands in sharp contrast to Morley's Parnassus. The bookseller Henry Earlforward is a miser. His refusal to waste money on heating, medicine or even food leads to the death of both his wife and himself. It is a tragic story of failure and failed hopes. The location of the shop is described as 'outworn shabbiness, grime and decay' and the store itself appeals to those 'ravenously desiring to get something for much less than its real value' (Bennett 1923, 4). Earlforward's wife ceases her attempts to clean the shop when her husband explains that buyers are attracted by darkness and dinginess as signs of bargains within (Bennett 1923, 118).

The publication in 1931 of the anonymous *Private Papers of a Bankrupt Bookseller* followed this theme of failure. According to the fictional metanarrative of the book, the papers were found by a draper when he took over the bookstore. This future bankrupt begins his business with great hopes and an optimistic view of literature that rivals Roger Mifflin's own:

> I am a bookseller. I am not a bookseller born and bred. I am one who came late to the craft, but, if late, not less lovingly.

> Books are a transcription of life, they say, but to me they are
> more than the transcript. They are Life itself, for as it was in the
> beginning – is now – and ever shall be, 'in the beginning was
> the Word'. (Darling 1931, 13)

The cold facts of the book business gradually weigh him down, however, and his faith in literature and his trust in readers lead him to business failure: 'That frivolous young widow', he opines, 'ought to have paid for the solaces she declared so often she found in books' (Darling 1931, 303). His neighbour sees it differently, describing him as a poor businessman with 'absurd ideas'; 'I heard him refusing to sell a book', the neighbour writes in a foreword, 'because he said he wanted it for himself' (Darling 1931, 7). To escape his creditors, the bookseller considers burning the store or disappearing into the night, but, at last, he chooses suicide. His neighbour explains:

> They were going to sell him up and he was found in his back
> shop with his head lying on a cushion on the gas stove. The
> gas was full on and not lighted. The stove was one of the
> new kind – more like an ordinary grate than the upright sort.
> (Darling 1931, 8)

The fictional papers were published anonymously by William Y. Darling, a draper who, ten years later, would become an MP.

George Orwell contributed further dark impressions of British bookselling a few years later in *Keep the Aspidistra Flying* (1936). Gordon Comstock, an advertising copywriter, wishes to forgo the middle-class life of comfort. He refuses to be one of those who 'settle down, to Make Good, to sell your soul for a villa and an aspidistra'. To avoid the comfort of money 'he would refuse the whole business of "succeeding"; he would make it his especial purpose NOT to "succeed"' (Orwell 1936, 38). His choice of location for avoiding success is a bookshop; when he fails to not succeed well enough there, he moves to a worse bookstore. The stores themselves are described as small, dark and 'smelling of dust and decayed paper'. The books are 'mostly aged and unsaleable', looking 'like the tiered coffins in common graves' (Orwell 1936, 2).

The contrast with fictional bookstores in America was stark during this period. New York's famous Book Row started attracting used bookstores in 1890 and by the 1920s and 1930s was firmly established with dozens of stores operating within seven square blocks of Fourth Avenue (Mondlin and Meador 2005). This was also the golden age of detective fiction (James 2013) and Book Row provided the location for at least three mystery novels. The first was the *Colfax Book-Plate*, published in 1926 and serialized for the Western Newspaper Union between June and November 1928. The narrator is one Constance Fuller who works at Darrow's New and Second-Hand Bookshop on Fourth Avenue. Darrow's is a staid and well-run establishment and Constance spends much of the narrative trying to return to her cataloguing duties. As described by Constance, the store stands in sharp contrast to Riceyman's 'grim and decay':

> Every new customer coming in past my desk beside the front door gasps at the noble spread of the book-shelves from floor to ceiling on the long north and south walls, with a gallery running around them at half their height. He will find fiction on the tables, standard works on the walls, classified subject collections in the alcoves. He may view at leisure the fine collections of old prints and engravings which ornament the gallery railings and in which we do a considerable business. (Miller 1928, 11)

When a rare *Colfax Book-Plate* comes to the shop, it is quickly followed by death in the stacks of the store. The investigation takes place amid the bookstore work and the lives of the staff. In spite of the murder, the store continues its business and achieves unexpected successes due to Constance's efforts. The books themselves, and the *Book-Plate* in particular, provide the links between the characters that resolve the mystery.

Murder in the Bookshop (1936) and *Fast Company* (1938) were both penned by established writers of detective fiction. Carolyn Wells had written forty-four Fleming Stone mysteries between 1909 and the detective's appearance in *Murder in the Bookshop*. Wells based the bookshop in which the murder occurs on the Sign of the Sparrow, a basement bookstore on Book Row run by bookseller Alfred F. Goldsmith, with whom Wells had previously co-authored *A Concise Bibliography of the Works of Walt Whitman* (Wells and Goldsmith 1922). Goldsmith also provided the basis for the novel's bookseller John Sewell, 'most knowledgeable of all the dealers in the city' (Wells 1936, chap. 1). Sewell's bookstore is glorified by Wells 'as a place where one feels a shyness in the presence of books':

> Books you'd forgotten and books you wished you had forgotten. Rare books and always genuine. Queer books, holy books and poems by the Sweet Singer of Michigan. But all these things were in the great front room. There was a smaller room back of it, where the more nearly priceless volumes were kept in safes, and where conferences were held that often proved John Sewell's right to the title awarded him as most knowledgeable of all the dealers in the city. (Wells 1936, chap. 1)

Patrons of the store are wealthy and educated. They are 'connoisseurs and collectors' who gather to 'discuss bookish themes' (Wells 1936, chap. 1). The store and its patrons are a far cry from the miserable Mr McKechnie's bookstore that Orwell described in the same year, even with a dead body in the backroom.

In *Fast Company*, the booksellers start to take a more active role in the detections. The novel is written by Harry Kurnitz under the pseudonym of Marco Page. Kurnitz would later write one of the Thin Man films (*The Thin Man Goes Home*) and *Fast Company* follows the Thin Man formula. It features a husband and wife, Joel and Garda, who (like Nick and Nora Charles from Thin Man novels and films) maintain witty banter while solving the murder of a hated New York book dealer. Joel works as a bibliographic detective, recovering valuable stolen books for insurance companies. The plot revolves around the alterations of stolen volumes that he detects. It emulated *The Thin Man* effectively enough that M-G-M purchased the rights to the novel and brought Kurnitz in to write the screenplay. It successfully filled a gap in *The Thin Man* series and was followed by two more adventures for the book dealers, mining the same vein of humorous repartee amid crime and danger.

In both *Fast Company* and *Murder in the Bookshop*, the motive is money. The murdered book collector in Wells' mystery was on the verge of purchasing a book worth as much as $100,000 (twice the value of the 1911 auction price for the Gutenberg Bible). In *Fast Company*, Joel and Garda uncover a forgery scam in the heart of the rare book business in New York. The events in both bibliomysteries occur amid wealth. Joel and Garda, in spite of having to do recovery work to pay the bills, live a lavish lifestyle among the wealthy in New York. Philip Balfour, the victim found murdered in the bookshop, leaves behind a substantial estate and a book collection worth killing for.

Although the two versions of the book trade differ substantially in their reputations, both are presented positively; the trade itself is respectable or at least profitable. There is no bankruptcy, poverty, failure or death. The Robert Hoe auction marked the rise of New York and America as the location where bookselling could be presented as both glamourous and respectable and the novels reflect that rise.

Travelling Bookstores

In the summer of 1921 Frank Shay, proprietor of Frank Shays Bookshop in Greenwich Village, filled a Ford station wagon with $1,200 worth of books and headed to Cape Cod in search of customers vacationing there. The venture met with mixed success. On the first day he was ordered away from a wealthy-looking hotel that did not like peddlers and when he found a more tolerant beach crowd, he received a court summons for peddling without a license. The judge turned out to be a bibliophile who threw out the case and requested a chance to view the books for sale. Shay notes in his memoir of the trip that the judge did not worry about the cost of the books: 'No, he only remarked that such an opportunity to buy the books he wanted came so seldom he felt he had a right to splurge.' In spite of this one success, he did not earn enough to cover the costs. 'After the first thrill of seeing a travelling bookshop the natives left us severely alone. Selling books from a wagon is a good deal like selling a cure-all from the wagon of a medicine show' (Shay 1924).

Shay's travelling bookshop was a handsome Ford station wagon that had its name painted clearly on the sides: Frank Shay's Traveling Book Shop:

Parnassus on Wheels. It was christened before its journey began by Christopher Morley, author of a short book about another travelling book shop, *Parnassus on Wheels* (1917). Morley tells the story of a woman, Helen McGill, living with her brother, a farmer and successful author, in the New England countryside. When itinerant bookseller Roger Mifflin arrives and tries to sell Helen books, she chooses instead to buy the shop: a bookstore wagon drawn by a horse named Pegasus. She sets off immediately with Roger selling books to local country people.

Helen is not literary, but she likes a good book. She can see the commercial potential in selling books, the way she might have seen it in selling some other commodity. In contrast to her practicality, Roger Mifflin is a fanatic. He believes in the power of the written word to raise a person beyond the daily rigours of life. When his wagon arrives in a village, his sales pitch claims that books on a shelf make a man a better husband, a better father and a better citizen. Mifflin loves the books not as desirable objects in themselves, but as excellent tools to improve the human condition. He tells Helen, who has now purchased his travelling store, that 'when you sell a man a book you don't sell him just twelve ounces of paper and ink and glue – you sell him a whole new life. Love and friendship and humour and ships at sea by night – there's all heaven and earth in a book, a real book I mean. Jiminy!' (Morley 1917, 44).

The story of Helen, Roger and Helen's brother Andrew was inspired in part by *Adventures in Contentment*, a collection of short stories by the historian Ray Stannard Baker, writing under the pseudonym of David Grayson. Baker's book also features a literary bachelor and his unmarried sister, this time situated living an idyllic life on a New England farm. Baker's sister Harriet, like Helen, cares for him and is generally taken for granted (Baker 1922). Morley, in a letter to David Grayson which prefaces his own *Parnassus on Wheels*, notes that the Helen narrating this story 'used to mutter something about "Adventures in Discontentment" and ask why Harriet's side of the matter was never told?'[1]

---

[1] Morley (1979), *Parnassus on Wheels*. The letter prefacing the first editions of the novel is commonly left of subsequent editions, including Lippincott's 1945 republication and the Everyman Library edition of 1931. The version identified here is from the Gutenberg Project version (www.gutenberg.org/ebooks/5311).

This time it is Helen who is telling the tale, not the literary brother. In Grayson's version of events, the bookseller comes to the farm to sell a book subscription: *Living Selections from Poet, Sage and Humourist* (volume 1 of 6, including more than 1,162 pages and weighing in excess of ten pounds). Grayson, the literate farmer, takes the opportunity to teach the peddler that the true value of the book is not the object but the ideas within. Then he sends him on his way. Helen turns this lesson on its head: '[M]y line is common sense rather than literary allusions' (Morley 1955, 56).

Helen insists that she is practical and without literary interests, although 'human enough to like a good book' (Morley 1955, 28). She is thirty-nine years of age and keeps house for her farmer/author brother. Her brother's biographer describes her as a 'rural Xantippe' and 'the domestic balance-wheel that kept the great writer close to the homely realities of life'. When the book peddler arrives, the author/brother is away on literary work. In this scenario, it is the peddler who idolizes literature and the sister, left to her own devices, sees the value in the book as a business as she rides off with Mifflin.

Discovering independence through a travelling bookstore was repeated in Valerie Baxter's *Shirley: Young Bookseller* (1956), a volume in the Bodley Head Career Book for Girls series published in 1950s' England. It tells the story of Shirley Dixon, a twenty-two-year-old woman in England who 'became a bookshop assistant quite by chance' (Baxter 1956, book blurb). Like Helen, she feels trapped in her home and her family expectations.

Her opportunity to escape comes, as it did for Helen, in the arrival of a collection of books (westerns, crime and detective novels). This time it is an academic great-uncle who dies and leaves his library to her father, who does not want them. The van is provided by a friend with whom she is due to take a caravanning holiday; the friend suggests they have some fun peddling the books to farmhouses as they travel.

Shirley's bookselling adventure is meant to provide a lesson and induce the reader to consider bookselling as a profession. Shirley is without literary conceits or ambitions. The farm customers the women visit show a natural desire for entertainment and a passion for reading. Shirley sells all her detective novels to the men on the farms and all the westerns to schoolboys in a village fair. Her used books are commodities and she prices them at a sharp discount of 'five for half a crown' (Baxter 1956, 38). She realizes early on that stopping at a farmhouse door and asking if they want books won't work; instead, she quickly develops a tray of samples to bring with her.

She also learns the important lesson that books allow her access to the social lives of her customers. During her ten days selling from the caravan, she meets a farmer and his family, helps a woman whose young child has cut itself, a young housewife whose husband has invited the boss over for dinner on the day the cook quit and a wealthy socialite needing help with a village fair. Not all these encounters end in sales, but Baxter has Shirley consider after each encounter what book might have sold had it had been in the car. Books, not necessarily literature but books as entertainment or information, are needed in these rural locations. The person who supplies them will have the opportunity for glimpses into families and communities. Bookselling, even for an itinerant bookseller travelling around the English or New England countryside, is a business grounded in the local community.

The romance of a travelling bookstore is brought into a twenty-first century context in Jenny Colgan's *The Bookshop on the Corner* (2016) (published as *The Little Shop of Happy-Ever-After* in the UK). Nina is a librarian who was recently made unemployed when the library was converted to a media hub. Although she persuades the library to donate its stock of books to her, she has no idea what to do with them and simply stores them in the house. Selling the books is the obvious solution, but she has no resources for starting a bookstore. Unlike Helen and Shirley, Nina is not trapped in a family relationship of any sort. She has friends but they are supportive of her, rather than dependent on her. What she lacks is a business background, financial support and confidence. She has been made redundant and told that her profession, that of librarian, is no longer needed.

When she reads about Sarah Henshaw's success selling books from a canal barge (Henshaw 2014b), she has the idea of buying a van and selling the books from there. She finds an advertisement for a used van in Scotland and swiftly buys a bus ticket to the remote fictional town of Kirrenfief. Like Helen and Shirley, she travels to a bucolic, rural landscape and finds people in need of books. The world has changed, however, with the internet and television. Her potential customers, although living in isolated farmsteads and communities, have full access to a range of entertainment and information. There is no longer a need for a book to supply these things, as it had been in New England in 1917 or middle England in the 1950s. With the advent of eBooks and e-commerce, books and bookstores are as close as the computer screen.

Nina's arrival in the remote village is treated with amusement or distrust and the idea of the book van is a local joke. However, like Shirley before her, Nina uses the books as an access point into people's lives. Although Nina has no shared background of experience with the people there, the books do. Because she has read a book about an experience, she can recognize the needs of locals. She recognizes the need in the local shop owner who had refused to welcome her into the community:

> She looked at Lesley, who worked crazy hours, who lived above the shop, seemingly on her own, who always seemed angry about how life had turned out. She wondered. 'Try this', she said gently, handing over a copy of *The Heart Shattered Glass*. (Colgan 2016, 230)

This [fictional] book mirrors the woman's problems and personal history and the two women bond over the shared understanding. The value of the book van is not from the entertainment or information it provides. The value comes from Nina's knowledge of books, her ability to listen to what people say and to connect the book with the person. Rather than a book curator, she is a book apothecary. This is a profession that other booksellers will claim as well, most deliberately in Nina George's *The Little Paris Bookshop* (2017).

All three of these travelling booksellers – Helen, Shirley and Nina – set out as booksellers to gain independence, freedom and personal control of their lives. Each achieves this freedom and independence by cutting off their ties to a specific location. They bring their bookstores to the locations where they are needed and adapt to the local surroundings. Each of these booksellers also ends her travels in the same way: living with a male partner in a bricks-and-mortar bookstore. At the end of her adventure in *Parnassus on Wheels*, Helen has fallen in love and married Roger and the two of them have returned to her brother on the farm. Nina likewise falls in love (with her farmer-landlord), and moves into the farmhouse (although still selling books from her van). Shirley's bookselling adventures end differently. She sells all her 600 books and returns home to her former life. But, in good career guidance fashion, she quickly discovers a market for her new found skills and takes a job in the local bookstore. Shortly after that, she falls in love with a customer, the bookseller dies and she and her new boyfriend buy the store, renovate it and run it successfully with her (now) husband in charge and her as his invaluable assistant.

Shirley gets no sequel, but both Helen and Nina are more fortunate. The *Haunted Bookshop* (1919) finds Helen and Roger Mifflin running a used bookstore in Brooklyn. Helen has moved out of the business and has reassumed the role she played for her brother. She is mostly a non-entity in the story. In *The Bookshop on the Shore* (2019), Nina is pregnant and unable to maintain the van, so she must also move into a fixed bookstore. Her husband stays on the farm. The story this time revolves around another woman using the book van to escape a difficult life and gain her independence. Hers is another cosy romance and she ends her tale with a spouse and a ready-made family to raise.

The narrative structure of each of these novels begins with a woman whose personal options are constrained. Each woman has limited financial or social resources, so for each, the travelling bookstore is an affordable escape plan. Each woman discovers they have the financial common sense to run a small business, each one finds that bookselling provides a way to engage with people and join a community. And each one eventually ends their travels and gains a fixed, traditional abode for themselves, their loved ones and their businesses.

The narrative structure matches that of the real-life Sarah Henshaw (the putative inspiration for Nina's book van), who launched a book barge in 2009. With money borrowed from family, she purchased a sixty-feet-long narrowboat and refitted it as a bookstore and moored it at a local marina. By spring 2011 the enterprise was failing, so Henshaw chose to lose the mooring and travel the UK's inland waterways. At the end of her travels, she once again moored the barge, this time as a successful store and venue. The record of her travels on the book barge was published in 2014 as *The Bookshop that Floated Away*.

Henshaw describes her venture as an attempt to escape a difficult personal and financial situation, but also to gain independence from the major book retailers. She instigates a barter system for her books, asking people to provide 'milk, meals or amusement' in exchange for the value of books. As a media-savvy journalist, she alerts potential customers to her arrivals and lets them know of anything she might need, such as haircuts or marine support for the barge. 'For the last two years, I'd been bemoaning the unfair playing field from which independent booksellers compete against online and supermarket retailers to lure in cost-conscious customers. An experiment like this, I thought, could be a useful corrective to the easy acceptance that value for money has just one currency' (Henshaw 2014a).

Like her fictional predecessors, the selling of books allows her access into the lives of a disparate group of people, although unlike them she kept mainly to more populated parts of the country, including a spell in London. The end of her journey finds her back where she began, once again moored in the marina (although she has since relocated the barge to Burgundy, France).

If it is true, as Edward Casey argues, that 'places not only are, they happen' (Casey 1996), then places have an energy that is intrinsic to them. Energy is required to keep things happening. But energy is always in a limited supply and must be generated. As these bookstore locations keep changing, and as the locale of the stores shifts to meet the context of the new locations, energy of some sort must be expended. The bookseller is, as Buzbee writes, 'a groundskeeper concerned with the order and care and stock of that space' (Buzbee 2008, 105) constantly working and expending energy to maintain the space. Nina, Shirley, Helen, and Sarah all find that their journeys must come to an end as they shift the energy of bringing books to communities toward building a community through their bookstores.

National Identities

The bookseller working in Leonardo Padura's *Havana Fever* has no bookstore. The main character, Mario Conde ('the Count'), was a homicide detective in Havana in the 1970s and 1980s. His final year on the force, 1989, is recorded in Padura's *Four Seasons Cycle: Havana Blue* (2007), *Havana Gold* (2008), *Havana Red* (2005) and *Havana Black* (2006). At the end of that year, Conde became a bookseller in a city ravaged by what Padura's characters call 'the crisis', a lengthy period of shortages and austerity that 'dwarf all previous versions', hitting even 'the venerable world of books':

> Within a year publishing went into freefall, and cobwebs covered the shelves in gloomy bookshops where sales assistants had stolen the last light bulbs with any life, that were next-to useless anyway, in those days of endless blackouts. Hundreds of private libraries ceased to be a source of enlightenment and bibliophilic pride, or a cornucopia of memories of possibly happy times, and swapped the scent of wisdom for the vulgar, acrid stench of a few life-saving banknotes. (Padura 2003, 14)

The former detective now works as a book scout, wandering through this austere landscape seeking books to purchase and sell to buyers in the United States and elsewhere (but rarely in Cuba). When he sees a likely looking old mansion, he knocks on the door 'asking whoever opened up if they were interested in selling a few well-worn books' (Padura 2003, 15).

Like Roger Mifflin, he values books as a medium for the culture of his country. *Havana Fever* is full of Conde's detailed bibliographic descriptions of antiquarian works published in Cuba. On occasion, when he discovers a book that he recognizes as an important part of Cuba's heritage, he advises book owners against selling the book (even if they are selling to be able to buy food). He has ceased to sell books from a market stall because selling the literature of Cuba 'fanned smouldering remains of ravaged pride' (Padura 2003, 15).

Havana in the 1990s is a different world from the 1919 New England landscape in which Mifflin worked. People are disillusioned and hungry. 'Now we're halfway round the track', a friend opines to Conde, 'and are going blind, as well as bald and cirrhotic, and there's not all that much we want to see anymore' (Padura 2003, 160). People are starving. Jon Lee Anderson, in a 2013 interview with Padura, described the historical situation. The Soviet Union was collapsing, along with its financial aid, and American blockades were strengthening:

> Because of the lack of fuel, bicycles replaced cars, and oxen replaced tractors. Many Cubans went hungry; a Party official confessed to me that his family sometimes had little more than sugar water for dinner. Violence, theft, and prostitution soared, and there were riots in poor neighbourhoods. (Anderson 2013)

The bookstores of Conde's Havana are market stalls and backrooms. The Count has no fixed bookstore location. Unlike Roger Mifflin and the other travelling bookstores, he lacks even a wagon or barge. He depends on his friends and book dealing associates, many of whom have been his close friends since childhood. The customers seldom live in Cuba, and the books that are sold often leave the country. There are several crimes in the novel, including drug-running, prostitution and murder; Conde, however, when he discovers a fantastic library of rare Cuban books, suspects that he is committing what might be the gravest crime of all:

> Knowing that three generations of a Cuban family had devoted money and effort to that wondrous array of close to 5,000 volumes, that had travelled half the globe in order to find a place in these bookcases which were immune to damp and dust, seemed like an act of love he was now mercilessly destroying. Most painful of all was the certainty that profanation would lead to chaos and that chaos often sparked off the collapse of the most solid of systems. Wasn't his presence helping to verify that equation? His hands and economic interests were violating something sacred, and the Count anticipated his deed would provoke a chain reaction he still couldn't imagine, but which was imminent. (Padura 2003, 132–3)

Questions of place and power permeate the novel. Cuba had avoided the modern 'compression of space-time' articulated by David Harvey in *The*

Condition of Postmodernity. Harvey argued that capitalism, through a range of technologies, 'annihilates space through time' (Harvey 1990, 46). Harvey defines communication and movement as the defining factors of the modern experience of time-space (and hence of place); Doreen Massey adds 'dimensions of control and initiation' as factors that define this compression. She points out that 'the ways in which people are inserted into and placed within "time-space compression" are highly complicated and extremely varied' (Massey 2012, 62).

In Padura's novel, Cuba has avoided the time-space compression that Harvey describes. In Cuba, capitalism and technology have not eliminated distance or obscured borders. Padura shares Massey's scepticism about the power of capitalism to compress time and space; like Massey, he emphasizes the specifics of the location and the locale in this process. He makes it clear that this type of time-space compression is reserved for the nations that have gained political and economic power through capitalism. In Cuba, the disorientation that Harvey describes as caused by this compression is replaced by other forms of unease and dissatisfaction. Padura is himself a part of what he calls the 'hidden generation': the Cubans who came of age after the worst spasms of the revolution but before the fall of communism. He puts his experience into the mouth of Conde's friend Rabbit, who complains that 'Life was passing us by on all sides':

> [A]nd to protect us they gave us blinkers like mules. We should only look ahead and stride towards the shining future awaiting us at the end of history and, obviously, we weren't allowed to get tired on that road. Our only problem was the future was very far off and the path went uphill and was full of sacrifices, prohibitions, denials and privations. The more we advanced, the steeper the slope and more distant the shining future, which was fading quickly anyway. [...] I sometimes think they dazzled us with all that glare and we walked past the future and didn't even see it. (Padura 2003, 160)

This disillusion makes Conde's passion for the books of his country more powerful; it becomes the driving force in all he does. When he discovers a library collected before the revolution and maintained, but never altered or read, by the children of its founder, his response is both commercial and cultural. He recognizes that these books will make him a fortune as he sells them, but he also realizes a responsibility to his country to keep the books in Cuba. He agrees to sell the volumes for the library owners, but only if they agree to allow him to set the most valuable aside to remain in Cuba.

These books provide Conde with a personal form of time-space compression. The books he finds are not mainly literature, great works of writing that can be easily reproduced. They are physical editions of books such as Miró Argenter's *Chronicles of the War in Cuba* (the 1911 princeps edition); Antonio Bachiller y Morales' *Notes Towards the History of Letters and Public Education on the Island of Cuba* (1859); the *Alphabetical Index of Demises in the Cuban Liberation Army* by Major-General Carlos Roloff (the rare 1901 single printing in Havana); *Notes Towards the History of Letters and Public Education on the Island of Cuba*; the cookbook *My Pleasure? An indispensable ... culinary guide* (illustrated by Conrado Massaguer) (Padura 2003, 30). These books are valued as editions, as individual objects of desire to be admired for their aesthetic qualities as well as their historical and cultural value. They include histories, cookbooks, ornithology, economic and scientific texts, as well as the more literary novels and poetry.

Conde values them for their ability to connect him with his country's past. This connection is symbolized by a magazine photograph of a 1950s' bolero singer, the search for whom will provide an essential thread in his investigations when the library owner is murdered. The photograph was stored by someone thirty years earlier between the pages of a cookbook. The murder itself is motivated by connections created by the books and the secrets those connections reveal. In the conclusion, the mystery is resolved by another discovery found among the books of the library. These books are relics of a better past and are a cultural legacy. They are also physical conduits to that past that bring old knowledge and emotions into the present.

The Count is unable to protect this legacy. He is a bookseller without a bookstore. Lacking a location to cultivate, he cannot gather; he cannot create a sense of place. He has no space in which to build a dam against the changes that are happening. He is unable to build. Throughout the novel he travels through Havana, like Bloom in Dublin, seeing, noticing, investigating and experiencing. He does not, however, create. Even the selling of his books is done behind closed doors on the black market. He recalls the library of his school and the school librarian, Lame Cristóbal, who instilled in him his love of books. He returns to the school fifteen years later to find Cristóbal's library destroyed:

> To his eternal grief, the ex-student had had to acknowledge that Lame Cristóbal's fears had been surpassed. A few battered, moribund books were dozing among the empty spaces on the once packed shelves, whence Greek and Latin classics, tragic Englishmen and Italian poets, chroniclers of the Indies and Cuban novelists and historians had flown their nest. The plundering had been merciless and systematic, and apparently nobody had been held responsible for the vandalism. (Padura 2003, 133)

While Cristóbal lived and worked in the library, he maintained a location for the books and the literature. Chaos reigns without such a location or its protector.

Conde's story continues into 2021 with the last volume to date, *The Transparency of Time*. Facing his sixtieth birthday, Conde looks back on a life he describes as a failure. 'Conde had spiralled down a dark tunnel as dealing in used books became ever less profitable – to the extent that he was even thinking about repurposing himself and finding another way to survive, like some of his colleagues were doing' (Padura 2021, 25). Without a location, without being able to create a space to gather books, customers, readers, practices and history, he cannot protect that which he values most.

The two booksellers at the centre of *The Book Hunters of Katpadi* (2017) have a similar passion and mission. Neelambari Adigal (Neela) and her associate, Kayalveli Anbuchelvan (Kayla), run the bookstore Biblio: Antiquarian, Fine and Rare Editions in Chennai, India. Neela learned the book trade in London and developed a substantial collection before returning to India with a vision:

> Neela's vision was to coax an antiquarian culture from these
> exchanges – inspire Indian bibliophiles to embrace the book
> arts; identify serious collectors; involve book scholars; initiate
> a pukka antiquarian book fair and form a bibliophile club
> along the lines of the Roxburghe Club in London or the
> Grolier Club in New York. Her high standards for the book-
> shop had made it possible for Biblio to become a member of
> the International League of Antiquarian Booksellers (ILAB)
> within a year of its existence. (Sebastian 2017, 75–6)

The novel is a celebration of antiquarian book collecting, presenting India
as a country with a bibliographic history that is rightfully now being
celebrated. The only real villain in the story is Viscount Ricky
Pilkington, 'a rich, titled revisionist scholar who plans to build a museum
showcasing, in his words, "the glory of the British Raj"' (Sebastian 2017,
45). Unlike all the other characters in *Katpadi*, his interests are ulterior to
those of India.

The store that Neela creates is designed to welcome anyone passionate
about books. It is purposefully designed to be unlike the layout of any other
existing Indian used bookstore:

> Neela knew that an antiquarian bookshop that served the
> serious book collector couldn't afford to have books lying
> around in joyful chaos. Biblio's stock of rare, fine and first
> editions, displayed in glass-enclosed bookcases, were meticu-
> lously stocked and beautifully arranged. (Sebastian 2017, 8)

Instead of an overflow of books, Biblio's stock is meticulously displayed in
glass cabinets or beautifully arranged shelves. 'The first thing you saw was
a riot of pulpy, lurid colours – the bright yellows and reds and greens and
oranges of vintage paperbacks, displayed face-up because they were collected for their cover art' (Sebastian 2017, 8). By design, the space of the
store attracts book lovers (wealthy and poor) and scholars in equal measure.

In many ways, Biblio is a London antiquarian store transported to
Chennai. Neela's training was in London and she has brought that

antiquarian book trade knowledge into the context of India. An entire chapter of the novel, 'A Fine Movable Type', is devoted to a lecture Neela gives on antiquarian book collecting in India, explaining why the tradition had not developed there as it had in other countries. The reasons have to do with the nature of the book in India and how it had developed from other traditions. This process echoes arguments made by R. Mantena in her analysis of the work done by British eighteenth-century antiquarians in India, which notes that their 'local assistants' (which Mantena refers to as 'intellectuals') brought their own practices of history to the work, creating with their British counterparts a new historical method. 'The emergence of new practices of history', she contends, 'was conditioned by the *encounter* between British and Indian intellectual practices' (Mantena 2012, 5). Neela is likewise attempting to change the practices of bibliographic heritage and culture by bringing Indian understanding to the fore.

She is both more ambitious than Conde in Cuba and more successful. Conde only wants to preserve the past; Neela is using her store to control that past. Because she has the funding and the location, she can work with other local institutions, such as the local book auction house, binders and typesetters. She is also able to build. She establishes a bibliographic society (the Ziegenbalg), antiquarian book catalogues and the first antiquarian book fair in Chennai. She has a location where she can be found and has designed it as a gathering place for like-minded bibliophiles.

The potential power of a bookstore – as a fixed location able to gather people and ideas together and achieve a common purpose, is evidenced differently in *The Stationery Shop* (Kamali 2019). Set in Tehran in 1953, the shop is run by Mr Fakhri who is a supporter of the government and Prime Minister Mohammad Mosaddegh. In the period building up to the coup that put the Shah in power, he allows the books in the shop to be used for hiding messages between those loyal to Mosaddegh. The system works if the messages can be trusted; it fails at a crucial moment in the story's main plot when a romantic tryst fails due to a break in the system.

Both Biblio and the Stationery Shop succeed in their goals because they have a fixed location and present a particular face to the world. Visitors know where the store is located and they understand what to expect when they arrive. Thus, the stores gather particular people with specific, often common, goals and perspectives. In both narratives, the bookstore acts as seedbeds for the communities.

Permanence defines the two bookstores that dominate the multiple, intertwining narratives of Carlos Ruiz Zafón's literary series The Cemetery of Forgotten Books. The story of Barcelona and the Sempere family of booksellers begins in *The Shadow of the Wind* (2002), extends backwards with *The Angel's Game* (2008), moves forward again in *The Prisoner of Heaven* (2012) and concludes with *The Labyrinth of the Spirits* (2018). The four novels weave back and forth in time between 1899 and 1975, concluding with a coda that brings the narrative up to the 1990s when Zafón was writing the novel. It is a tale of the telling of the past, of remembering the past to shape a future and as such is a part of Spain's 'memory boom' (Davis 2005; Meddick 2010; Simine 2013), a recovering of the memory of the Spanish Civil War's brutal reality that had been buried during Spain's *Pacto del Olvido* (Pact of Forgetting), a tacit agreement within Spain to forget the past to avoid opening old wounds, but a pact that may have buried rather than resolved that past (Davis 2005, 863).

The Barcelona in which Zafón places his bookstores is a gothic landscape of crumbling ruins, dark alleys, storms and mysteries. Among the gothic locations are Montjuïc Castle, where Civil War prisoners were tortured and executed, and the Aldaya Mansion, a crumbling building that houses some of the first novels most haunting scenes (Trotman 2007). The central gothic element in the narrative, one that provides a focal point for the characters' lives and the central metaphor for the series, is the labyrinthine Cemetery of Forgotten Books.

Isaac Monfort, the Cemetery's caretaker, describes it as a bookstore 'of sorts'. The protagonist and putative narrative of the first volume in the series, Daniel Sempere, is taken there just before his eleventh birthday by his father, owner of Sempere and Son, the other bookstore that grounds the series. Daniel's mother died when he was four; on the morning when the child wakes, crying because he cannot remember his mother's face, the father takes him to the Cemetery of Forgotten Books at five o'clock in the morning. 'Some things', his father explains, 'can only be seen in the shadows' (Zafón 2001, 2).

The shop is a labyrinth in the centre of Barcelona. Its age is uncertain and it may be as old as the city itself. It is filled with frescoes of angels and fabulous creatures, palatial corridors and labyrinthian passageways crammed with books. His father introduces Daniel to the mystery of what he describes as a sanctuary:

> Every book, every volume you see here, has a soul. The soul of the person who wrote it and of those who read it and lived and dreamed with it. Every time a book changes hands, every time someone runs his eyes down its pages, its spirit grows and strengthens. ... When a library disappears, or a bookshop closes down, when a book is consigned to oblivion, those of us who know this place, its guardians, make sure that it gets here. In this place, books no longer remembered by anyone, books that are lost in time, live forever, waiting for the day when they will reach a new reader's hands. (Zafón 2001, 3–4)

Richmond Ellis points out that the library is mythologized as 'the repository of all the books ever written and in a sense the nexus of all discourse' (Richmond Ellis 2006). If that is the case, then it is a discourse that has been buried in the crypt of this cemetery. According to Judith Meddick, it is 'imbricated with the politics of memory':

> It represents the 'crypt' that has been constructed within the psychic space of post-war Barcelona – an enclave which houses a silenced history in the ego of the city that has been designated unutterable by the discursive territory around it.
> (Meddick 2010, 252–3)

The Cemetery of Forgotten Books, however, is like any cemetery where the dead lie in wait for their resurrection. Daniel, peering through the shadows, sees his father's rare-book colleagues browsing the shelves, resurrecting books. Some of these volumes are destined to rise again and live within Sempere and Sons and the other bookstores in Barcelona.

Sempere and Son is the other bookstore that provides a fixed narrative location within the series. The store was founded by Daniel's great-grandfather and is currently run by his father. As the narrative progresses through the four volumes, Daniel takes over the store and he expects his son to do the same. Each Sempere father takes his son to the Cemetery, each father warns his son that 'you mustn't tell anyone what you're about to see today' (Zafón 2001, 1).

Sempere and Son specialize in rare collectors' editions and second-hand books. Young Daniel sees the shop as an 'enchanted bazaar' in which he makes friends in the pages of books (Zafón 2001, 1). Unlike the Cemetery, it is a 'classy establishment' that welcomes strangers through its doors. It is a place where books are remembered and shared. In the final volume of the series, it is where the community gathers to hear the announcement of Franco's death. Locals come there when they have problems. It is a central part of the local community, sharing the communal activity but not dominating it. It is defined by its normality.

Daniel Sempere is the main protagonist of *The Shadow of the Wind*, the first volume in the series which sets a framework that the following volumes must fit within. In it, he finds, during that first visit to the Cemetery in 1945, a book by the author Julián Carax. His fascination with that text leads him back to events leading up to and during the Spanish Civil War. Carax has disappeared and someone has been burning all copies of his books so that Daniel holds the only known remaining copy of his last book, titled *The Shadow of the Wind*. Six years after discovering the book, he notices a character from the novel watching him in the darkness. As the narrative progresses and moves back and forth across the early decades of the twentieth century in Spain, his own life becomes increasingly entwined with the history of Carax, Franco's fascist Spain, and the Cemetery of Forgotten Books.

The gothic landscape of the book has been noted frequently in studies of the text (Richmond Ellis 2006; Trotman 2007; Meddick 2010; Byron 2012; Aldana Reyes 2020). Meddick identifies the Cemetery, the Adaya mansion, and Montjuïc Castle as specific gothic locations, but the city itself is defined by mystery, horror and gloom. The bookstore of Sempere and Sons stands in contrast to the city due to its normality. The owner, Daniel's father Juan, is kind, patient and thoughtful. As the series develops, the power of his patience and love become obvious; he provides one of the two dependable pillars in Daniel's life. The other is the gothic character Firmen, who provides what Zafón has described as the 'moral centre' of the series, 'a very tragic character because he is a man who tries to be a better man than he is, while many of the characters are the opposite' (Stephens 2012). Firmen will end the series as the caretaker of the Cemetery of Forgotten Books and in many ways becomes the central protagonist of the story.

In an article in the *Cambridge Companion to Gothic Fiction*, Steven Bruhm argues that society needs the gothic to deal with the traumas of the past. Trauma, he argues, destroys narrative memory. Traumatic periods of history shatter our collective memory into multitudes, forcing us to 'confront our demons, our worst fears about the agents and influences that might control and create us'. This fragmentation renders 'humans unable to tell any kind of complete story about them'. The Gothic ravages history and fragments the past for meaning, 'meshing with our own investments now as we attempt to reinvent history' (Bruhm 2002, 274).

The Cemetery of Forgotten Books series is composed of fragments. Daniels's parentage is fragmented between Sempere Senior and a writer that his investigations uncover. His moral compass is fragmented between his father and Fermin. The landscape of Barcelona is fragmented by war and hidden animosities that he uncovers and reignites. The memory of Barcelona and Spain is fragmented by silence. The narrative structure of the novels themselves is fragmented, moving quickly between decades though remaining centred in Barcelona. The protagonist of *The Shadow of the Wind* is Daniel, but, as the series progresses, that too fragments as the series becomes the story of many people who experienced the Spanish Civil War and Franco's Spain. Even the authorship of the books becomes fragmented; at various stages authorship is attributed to Daniel Sempere, to Daniel's son Julián and to Julián Carax.

The first volume of the series set up a fragmented history and attempted to provide a structure for understanding it. The following volumes disrupted the happy ending it provided, only to provide another—more fully embracing though no less duplicitous. In the last chapter of *The Labyrinth of the Spirits*, Julián Sempere tells of how he came to write the Cemetery of

Forgotten Books series under the name of Julián Carax. All the narrative disjunctions are connected and explained with this final, false narrative in which Julián Sempere doubles for Carlos Ruiz Zafón.

Zafón needs Julián Carax and Julián Sempere the way Daniel needs Sempere Senior and Fermin, Bookstore and Cemetery, fragmented past and reliable present. Robert Richmond Ellis notes how these interdependencies play out in *The Shadow of the Wind:*

> Without Daniel (the Spanish present), Julián (the Spanish past) will irrevocably die. Conversely, without Julián, Daniel will lack the historical foundation necessary for the creation of a future of his own. Julián and Daniel are poised on opposite sides of a historical divide of such depth that rapprochement seems impossible. Yet their union (along with the union of the texts in which they are embedded and the generations they represent) is the implicit promise of the entire Ruiz Zafón narrative. (Richmond Ellis 2006, 846)

Likewise, Sempere and Sons' modern, community-facing bookstore requires the impossible store of the Cemetery of Forgotten Books. The Cemetery is a rabbit hole of the past, of failed bookstores and abandoned libraries, a store of memory to be mined. The Cemetery likewise requires Sempere and Sons (bookstore and book dealers) to resurrect the books and bring them back to the open air. In his first visit to the Cemetery in 1945, the ten-year-old Daniel sees his father's colleagues browsing the labyrinth. His father calls them the guardians of the Cemetery's books. Daniel, perhaps with more insight, describes them as alchemists as they curate the past into memory (Zafón 2001, 3).

The Fantastic

In a recent study of bookstore spaces (*The Spaces of Bookselling*), Kristin Highland suggests a typology of bookstores, dividing them into the 'intimate' and the 'monumental'. The locale of some bookstores is designed to be an 'intimate domesticized retreat removed from the insistent demands of modern time'. The corners, nooks and crannies designed into many book-stores provide refuges where people find pause, stillness, and comfort (Highland In Press). Roger Mifflin's New York store, Parnassus at Home, could be an example:

> The shop had a warm and comfortable obscurity, a kind of drowsy dusk, stabbed here and there by bright cones of yellow light from green-shaded electrics. There was an all-pervasive drift of tobacco smoke, which eddied and fumed under the glass lamp shades. Passing down a narrow aisle between the alcoves the visitor noticed that some of the compartments were wholly in darkness; in others where lamps were glowing he could see a table and chairs.
>
> (Morley 1923, 5–6)

Zafón's *Cemetery of Forgotten Books* offers a fictional version of the other type of store, which Highland terms the monumental. These are the locales frequently included in lists of the most beautiful or greatest bookstores in the world, lists which typically include 'the 17,000 square feet Taipei bookstore, Eslite Dunnan, the Livraria Lello in Porto, Portugal, with its sweeping staircase and neo-Gothic architecture, and Mexico City's soaring Cafebreria El Pendulo' (Highland in press). Highland emphasizes the 'discourse of sacred monumentality' informing these stores, which are often described as cathedrals or temples to the book; some, such as the Selexyz Dominicanen bookstore in the Netherlands, are former cathedrals (Highland in press).

In fiction as in architecture, the bookstore is often an access point to the fantastic. The Livraria Lello in Porto is among these monumental stores that provide fantastical spaces that border on the sacred. It is also famous as the putative source for the fictional and fantastical Flourish and Blotts in J. K. Rowling's Harry Potter series. (Brownfield 2020) The store itself is only briefly described in Rowling's books; she focuses instead on the magical books inside, including invisible books on invisibility and books about monsters that attack their readers. The store, however, features as part of Harry's entrance into the wizarding world. Once again, the bookstore is located on a border, this time one between the rational world and the magical one.

This borderline world is explored in several short story collections, including *Shelf Life* (2012), *The Magic Bookshop Trilogy* (2019), *The Haunted Bookshop and Other Apparitions* (2007), *Else Fine . . . Little Tales of Horror from Libraries and Bookshops* (2004) and *Books of the Weird* (2018). The last two are collections of stories by John D. Riley, long-time owner of a used bookstore in New England. The stories are a mix of fantasy, the macabre, and the comic, mostly set in bookstores or libraries. The story 'Orbis Pictus' (Riley 2004, 9–14) begins with a bibliophile eager to enter a bookstore that always appears to be closed when he passes by. He finally manages to enter the store and is given the opportunity of a lock-in while the gnomish owner runs an errand. To his dismay, he soon discovers that the books are all illustrated by the vanities and sins of the townspeople, including his own.

The bookstore as a border-space between reality and fantasy is explored in the stories collected by Greg Ketter for *Shelf Life*. When browsers enter the bookstores in these tales, they enter a world regulated not by physics or logic, but by the nature of the books within. The book buyer in 'Ballards Books', for instance, finds the books in that store contain the narratives of the lives he might have led but did not. In 'The Cheese Stands Alone' a motorist, looking to kill some time before a dinner engagement, stops at a bookstore with no sign, full of people standing still, quietly staring at the books in their hands but never turning the pages. Unable to resist the pull of the store, he enters to find that each of the browsers had found the knowledge they needed, that each had made a pact with the devilish owner for that knowledge and each would stay browsing forever.

The link between the book and its reader is expressed powerfully in P.D. Cacek's 'A Book, By Its Cover'. In this Holocaust tale, Yavin is a young Jew living in Poland, in a town recently ravaged by Nazis who murdered local people and burned the books in the local store. Yavin despises the owner of the bookstore after seeing him cry bitter tears when the books were burned. 'The old man had wept for his books, but not once so much as glanced at the body that was sprawled on the ground only a few feet away. And when he finally said Kaddish, it was for the books alone'

(Cacek 2002, 27). What the boy does not understand is that the bookseller has found a way to transform people into their favourite books. Thinking that he could save the village this way, the bookseller had begun transforming everyone into books, which he would then send to safety. The bookseller's despair at the burning of the books becomes clear.

Bookstores in these tales are dangerous places. Like the books they store, they act as portals to other worlds, often internal ones. They are liminal spaces that reveal truths and capture lives. It is a danger created by the power that exists on borderlands. In 'Escapes' by Nina Kiriki Hoffman, Branigans Bookstore is dangerous, but it employs its power to protect its browsers. The store has a 'Choose your own adventure' section in which customers can choose their own lives. When Sylvia comes to work there, she is hiding from an abusive boyfriend and the store welcomes her and protects her. When the boyfriend, Peter, finds her, the store acts:

> The pink carpet snapped up and wrapped around Peter. He
> screamed and dropped the remote. The carpet wrapped
> tighter until all that was visible of Peter was his head.
> A corner of the carpet stuffed itself into his mouth.
>
> (Hoffman 2002, 208)

While Peter is trapped by the store, Sylvia goes to the 'Choose your own adventure' section and, using a pen dipped in her blood, writes Peter out of her life forever.

The power of these bookstores comes from their position in the confluence of the real world and the world of the written word. Words in these stories have power. They may have the power to rewrite reality, as in 'A Book, By Its Cover' and 'Escapes'. They also have the power to store knowledge and truth. The bookstore contains these powerful objects and therefore has unnatural power that may trap or save the unaware browser, as happens in 'Orbis Pictus' and 'The Cheese Stands Alone'.

The American poet Robert Frost used this potential of the bookstore in his *Masque of Mercy* (1947). In this verse drama, the biblical Jonah seeks sanctuary from God in a bookstore where the store's Keeper is debating with St Paul. Along with the Keeper's wife, Jesse Bel, they debate mercy and justice amidst the books. Jonah is fleeing his role of prophet:

> I had the hall all hired,
> The audience assembled. There I was
> Behind the scenes ordained and advertised
> To Prophesy, and full of prophecy,
> Yet could not bring myself to say a word.
> I left light shining on an empty stage
> And fled to you. But you receive me not.
>   (Frost 1947, 35)

The debate ends after Paul and the Keeper have argued that Jonah's sense of justice is unreasonable. 'I should have warned you', Jonah answers, 'though my sense of justice was about all there ever was of me' (Frost 1947, 56). With that, he fades and speaks no more. Reason, which fills the bookstore's shelves, appears to have won out over faith. But the Keeper sees his own failure in Jonah's passing:

> My failure is no different from Jonah's.
> We both have lacked the courage in the heart to
>   overcome the fear with the soul
> and go ahead to any accomplishment.
>   (Frost 1947, 59)

The bookseller recognizes his fellowship with the prophet who sought shelter in the bookstore where St Paul, 'the fellow who theologized Christ almost out of Christianity' (Frost 1947, 36), keeps him company.

Recognizing the position of the bookstore on the border or written realities places responsibilities on the bookseller, more than many can handle. In Brian Stableford's 'The Haunted Bookshop', a colliery worker buys a used bookstore in Wales when the pits close and fills it with volumes from the colliery library. Believing the books themselves to be haunted, he hires a paranormal expert to excise the spirits. The expert in turn asks his book collecting, atheist friend to come along. The bookstore owner explains his that the haunting is not a ghost, not visible – it is only a presence felt when among the books.

The atheist book collector feels the presence as well and it is one he has felt before. After searching the colliery books for any items which he might want for himself, he describes the effect in words that echo those of Daniel in *The Shadow of the Wind*:

> I've only found a few, but they won't just sit on my shelves unread. I feel sorry for the rest, in a way. All that thought that went into their creation! All that effort! If they only had voices, they'd be clamouring for attention, don't you think? They'd be excited, wouldn't they, at having been taken out of their coffins at last and put on display? They probably thought that the Day of Judgement had come at last when Martin first unpacked them – but disillusionment must be setting in by now. How long do you think it takes a book to give in to despair? (Stableford 2001, 350)

The collector and the expert leave the book dealer Martin to his books, but Martin soon realizes he will never be a 'real bookman' and opens a newsagent or a pizza franchise.

Location and locale are elements of place that create the potential for meaning. The location of a bookstore in early twentieth century London or New York establishes a context and web of connections and trajectories, what Massey described as the potential 'arrangement-in- relation-to-each-other' that defines the space. Location, however, is not always physical. Bookstores exist in a metaphysical location as well. Amazon existed only in the cloud or on my Kindle long before it established any physical locations. Robert Frost's store exists somewhere between reason and mercy. Each of these bookstore locations is defined by its locale: what it looks like, how it is stocked and who visits or works there. Conde's book stock exists only in his mind and in the sources, travelling with him and having no fixed abode: locale, but no location. Sempere and the Cemetery are differentiated in their purposes by the very different ways they present themselves. The potential for the locations and locales of fictional bookstores to create a sense of place will be explored in the next section.

3 Sense of Place

If location and locale are the elements of place that create the potential for meaning, it is when they are enacted, or following de Certeau (1984) 'practised', that the potential is realized and a sense of place or identity is defined for the actors involved. In narrative theory, location and locale may be defined as the setting. Joshua Parker, in his paper on 'Conceptions of Place, Space and Narrative', while noting that narrative studies often conflate setting with the static concepts of background and description, argues for a more complex understanding of its role through a dynamic understanding of spatial identity. Referencing W.J.T. Mitchell's work on landscape, he notes that it works much like narrative as it encodes cultural values and meanings.

Yi-Fu Tuan's work on space and place (also referenced by Parker) makes the case for place as a 'pause'. 'If we think of space as that which allows movement then place is a pause; each pause in movement makes it possible for location to be transformed into place' (Tuan 1977, 6). Pause and movement create pattern and as such may be perceived as, or adapted to, narrative. It is these patterns of movement, pause, interactions and trajectories that enact John Agnew's sense of place (Agnew 2014). This section examines the bookstore as the site of this narrative landscape, examining two of the patterns created by that the enactment of the landscapes: safe havens and mysteries.

Safe havens

In Nina Hoffman's short story 'Escapes', Sylvia flees an abusive relationship. In Deborah Meyler's *The Bookstore*, the pregnant Esme has been abandoned by her wealthy boyfriend. Loveday, in Stephanie Butland's *Lost for Words*, is abandoned by her family. In Sheridan Hay's *The Secret of Lost Things*, Rosemary has to leave her homeland after the death of her mother. Each of these characters needs a haven, a place where they can find family and home, the type of place that Kristen Highland identified as one of the dominant bookstore tropes: 'intimate domesticized retreat removed from the insistent demands of modern time' (Highland in press).

The protagonists in these novels are widowed, divorced, orphaned and betrayed. Life has treated them harshly and the bookstore saves them from its harshness. Esme, the narrator of Deborah Meyler's *The Bookstore*, is a graduate student at Columbia University in love with a man from a wealthy family. She loves to slip into the Owl Bookstore in New York because of the community of people who work there:

> On Sundays the person in charge is a woman called Mary; she brings her dog with her, Bridget, a huge German shepherd. I would have thought that the presence of a large Alsatian simply could not encourage custom, but the contrary seems to be true. People rush in to see Bridget, and sometimes buy a book by accident. In the evenings there is a night manager called Luke who often wears a bandana. He is broad of shoulder and taciturn in aspect – he looks to be around thirty. When Luke is at the front counter at night, without George there, he sometimes has a guitar with him, and sits playing bits of tunes to himself. He nods in acknowledgment whenever I come in, but I can never think of anything much to say to him. (Meyler 2013, 6)

The store is her haven away from the pressures of graduate life. Later, when abandoned by the father of her unborn child, she retreats to that haven and the protection of the booksellers, George and Luke, who stand by her throughout her pregnancy. George is a bookseller in the mode of Roger Mifflin with 'the abstracted air of an old-fashioned scholar'. Obsessed with his bibliographic work, he frequently fails to notice what is happening around him; yet he is always solicitous and kind to Esme. He gives her work in the bookstore and supports her through the birth of her child.

The owner of the Yorkshire bookstore in *Lost for Words* is a similar type. Archie is kindly, wise, old-fashioned and lost within the world of his books. He makes corny jokes, smells of pipe-smoke, and watches over the young Loveday. He allows the store to remain in a constant state of disarray, depending on Loveday to look after its care and cleaning. When he saw the young Loveday steal a book, he offered to let her work off the price. The job at the store became her refuge when her father died and her family broke up. She finds security in the store when her boyfriend becomes obsessive and abusive. It is the place where she finds a new, more generous lover and it is where her mother finally finds her again.

These stores are small communities. The residents are the owners, the clerks, the customers and the books. As Lewis Buzbee has pointed out: 'A bookstore is for hanging out.' The bookstore, he continues, 'honours a public claim on its time and space' (Buzbee 2008, 4). As meaningful locations, they gather people who are welcome to browse and spend their leisure time. They are often classified among the 'third places' identified by Oldenburg as social spaces that provide an alternative to home and work. 'Third places exist outside the home and beyond the "work lots" of modern economic production. They are places where people gather primarily to enjoy each other's company' (Oldenburg 1989, 269).

They are also welcoming to those whom the community has abandoned. The Bright Ideas Bookstore, open until midnight, welcomes 'an entire world of *unidentified men*' as browsers. Apparently homeless, these men spend their days and evenings in the store, browsing the shelves and drinking the free coffee. Lydia, the clerk in the shop, calls them the Bookfrogs:

> To the inexperienced, many BookFrogs appeared as derelict or homeless, but to the seasoned eye it was clear that they'd shed themselves of the world, rejecting its costumes and rules in favor of paper and words. ... A few of the BookFrogs were so erudite that their rambling lessons in literature seemed easily as insightful as those that had come from her professors years ago in San Francisco, where she'd cobbled together an English degree. (Sullivan 2017, 18–19)

Lydia herself is escaping a past life of violence and pain. The Bright Ideas Bookstore gathers this damaged woman together with these unidentified men and the books they read, eventually forcing her to engage with her past and begin to repair the damage from which she has been hiding.

Tom Hope, a farmer in 1960s' Australia, is one of the two protagonists in *Bookstore of the Broken Hearted*. His wife abandoned him after a year of marriage, unable to tolerate life in the Australian outback. Desolated by the loss of his wife and ashamed to have been abandoned, Tom removes himself from the community in the town of Hometown, hiding at his farm and only travelling to town when necessary. Things change for him when a widow from Hungary arrives to start a bookstore. Hannah Babel asks for his help building the bookshelves and the sign for her store. Despite his scepticism about the value of a bookstore in his rural town, he agrees to help. She introduces him to books and he becomes enamoured with her passion for life and curious about the secret past she holds back. The bookstore provides both Tom and Hanna with a place where they can understand themselves and one another.

This narrative pattern is repeated in the cosy romance, *The Bookshop on the Corner*. Nina Redmond arrives in a remote Scottish town to start a travelling bookstore from a van. She rents a cottage from Lennox, a local farmer. Lennox's wife also abandoned him, also because she could not tolerate farm life in the countryside. Like Tom Hope, he helps her with her store (rescuing her van on several occasions), discovers that books have something to offer and becomes enamoured with the new bookseller in town.

At the outset of the novels, neither farmer understands the value of the bookstore for their community. When Tom Hope first sees the store while walking down the town's main street, he reacts in disbelief. '"This was to be a bookshop?" Tom murmured, "What the hell?" He couldn't prove it, but it was likely that not a half-dozen people in Hometown had ever opened the cover of a book' (Hillman 2018, 35). Hannah responds with confidence to Tom's concerns: 'They will read. They will come to Madame Babel' (Hillman 2018, 53). Nina also ignores her farmer's scepticism, her confidence boosted by the interest the local people show in her mobile bookstore.

In both cases, the bookseller herself is firmly committed to the venture. Nina may be unsure at the outset that a travelling bookstore is the best format, but she is firmly convinced of the value of books and the community's need. She is a literary matchmaker – she can identify the book any individual needs. And by doing so she helps not only the individuals but the community through which her van travels:

> Everyone was reading. People out in their gardens. An old lady in her wheelchair by the war memorial. A little girl absent-mindedly swinging on the swings, her feet dangling, completely engrossed in *What Katy Did*. In the baker, someone was laughing at a book of cartoons; at the coffee stand, the barista was trying to read and make someone a cappaciucino at the same time. Nina was amazed. It couldn't be – surely – that she had turned an entire town into readers. (Colgan 2016, 259)

The bookseller in *The Bookstore of the Broken Hearted* lacks Nina's gift for bibliotherapy, but not the conviction that she can make people want her books. She also has a more complex background than Nina, who was a librarian until the local council closed the library to make way for a media hub. Hannah is a survivor of the Holocaust in which she lost her husband and her son. The year is 1968 and she has come to the small Australian town of Hometown to open a bookstore as a gesture of defiance:

> Hannah had no sense of mission, no desire to convert the masses to art. But she kept count of the books she sold. Her target was twenty-five thousand, the approximate number of books burnt in Berlin on May 10th, 1933. (Hillman 2018, 195)

The novel moves between Tom's farm, Hannah's bookstore and Hannah's life as a Hungarian Jew before, during and after the war. The bookstore she opens in Hometown is her stand against all that has happened to her and her world. Before the war she was a musician from a well-educated family with a loving husband and a son. Although she survived the Holocaust, she lost both her husband and child. Finally able to return to her home in Budapest, she married again, only to lose her spouse to the Hungarian Revolution of 1956. For Hannah, the bookshop is a place to take a last stand. She invests all her money into the business, although as Tom points out it is almost certain to fail financially. In doing so, she finds some measure of solace but also brings hope to Tom and to his broken family.

Sara, who opens a bookstore in the town of Broken Wheel, Iowa, in Katarina Bivald's *The Readers of Broken Wheel Recommend* also does so as a gesture. She is a young woman from Sweden, eager to move beyond the limits of her hometown life. While working as a bookstore clerk in Sweden she starts up an unlikely penpal correspondence with the older Amy, a resident of the town of Broken Wheel in the American midwest. She comes for a visit to stay with Amy and talk books, only to find that Amy died the day before she arrived.

Broken Wheel takes its name from the fact that the first settlers stayed because their wagon broke down there. It is a small town that is slowly dying. The shops are mostly closed; only a café, grocery and bar are left. It is also a town where everyone knows everyone else's business and the residents know Sara is coming and insist she stay at Amy's now empty house until she is ready to return to Sweden.

Amy and Sara had connected through their common love of books and reading. Amy's house is full of her books. Sara, thinking about how to repay the townspeople for their kindness, realizes that 'this town was in desperate need of a bookstore' (Bivald 2013, 82). She decides to open a bookstore, using Amy's collection as a beginning stock. As she is on a tourist visa, she cannot work for the store, but she can volunteer as the owner and only employee.

Like Nina and Hannah, Sara's love of literature combines with natural empathy. She has the literary matchmaker ability to identify the right book for each person and discreetly begins to gain the locals' trust and friendship. The bookstore she creates transcends local prejudices and assumptions. She stocks gay romances to suit the owners of the local bar and soon has a local boy from the neighbouring (and more successful) town of Hope visiting to read them. She is even able to discretely persuade the town's most religiously conservative member to risk reading what she thought were morally corrupt books. The result is that the woman strikes up a relationship with a youth twenty years younger than she is. The town flourishes under the light that glows from the store's windows.

The Readers of Broken Wheel Recommend, like *The Bookshop on the Corner* and *The Secret of Lost Things*, is a 'cosy romance', a light read that moves inevitably toward a happy ending. Sara saves the town from its despair, the townspeople find a way to keep her and she and a local man (another a local farmer) find love. Her ridiculous enterprise and the books that she sells inspire other equally outlandish ones, until the final, and inevitable, happy endings. The final chapter title provides the scorecard:

> Epilogue: Happily Ever After (Books 4: Life 4. Final score: a draw). (Bivald 2013, 374)

Hannah opens her store as a challenge to the world that has tried to destroy all that she loved and valued. Nina, unemployed and outmoded, opens the mobile bookstore as an act of desperation. Sara's bookstore is an act of gratitude and an expression of hope. Each of these booksellers becomes a valued member of the rural community they join and each marries a local farmer.

Penelope Fitzgerald's *The Bookshop* is not a cosy romance and the outcome for bookseller Florence Greene is very different. She is a long-term member of the local community and is seeking not shelter but challenge:

> For more than eight years of half a lifetime she had lived at Hardborough on the very small amount of money her late husband had left her and had recently come to wonder whether she hadn't a duty to make it clear to herself, and possibly to others, that she existed in her own right.
>
> (Fitzgerald 1978, 1–2)

Like Nina, Hannah and Sara, Florence attempts to build a place for herself using her skills and abilities. She has faith in the intrinsic value of books and believes that their value can be the foundation for commercial success. She is a professional who worked in bookstores before she married and she understands the business. She has invested her life savings in the purchase of the store for her books and she intends to succeed. She clearly states the twin foundations of her beliefs—that books are valuable and that a store is a business— to her patronizing bank manager. When he condescendingly suggests that she is unprepared to run a business and that she is more interested in 'culture' than profit, she responds firmly: 'Culture is for amateurs. I can't run my shop at a loss. Shakespeare was a professional!' (Fitzgerald 1978, 6). Later, when he presents her with a nuisance lawsuit, she quotes John Milton:

> 'A good book is the precious life-blood of a master spirit, embalmed and treasured up on purpose to a life beyond life, and as such it must surely be a necessary commodity.
> (Fitzgerald 1978, 108)

Like Nina, Hannah and Sara, her bookshop is a success. She buys an empty building, stocks it with an inventory meant to appeal to the local population and responds to local needs with a lending library. When Nabokov's *Lolita* is published, she stocks 250 copies and, according to the local solicitor, her sale causes 'a temporary obstruction unreasonable in quantum and duration to the use of the highway' (Fitzgerald 1978, 150); in other words, it is so successful that the crowd around her window blocks the street.

Under Florence's professional direction, the shop flourishes commercially. However, everything about the shop is an affront to the establishment. Even her shelving defies hierarchy:

> The right-hand wall she kept for paperbacks. At 1s. 6d. Each, cheerfully coloured, brightly democratic, they crowded the shelves in well-disciplined ranks. They would have a rapid turnover and she had to approve of them; yet she could remember a world where only foreigners had been content to have their books bound in paper. The Everymans, in their shabby dignity, seemed to confront them with a look of reproach. (Fitzgerald 1978, 43–4)

Unlike her literary peers, Penelope ultimately stands alone in a town dominated by a monied family with cultural pretensions. The wealthy

Violet Gamart uses culture to claim social status for herself and to deny it to others. Her social position gives her influence and power that is denied to Florence. She sees Florence and her shop as an act of defiance against her absolute position of cultural authority. She makes use of the law, of local regulations, of the media, and of her political connections to deny success to the bookshop and establish an art studio in the building.

The Bookshop becomes a story of success denied. If the shop is an attempt to show that she 'existed in her own right', it becomes clear that this existence is an affront to others. Florence ends the story in bitter defeat. Mrs Gamart uses her social and political connections to force the closure of the store so the building can be used as a cultural centre. The townspeople do not rise to support her, neither is there any sense among them that the store was a place to be valued. She loses everything: her shop, the building, her books; even her car is taken by the bank.

The novel was made into a film in 2017 that leavens the bitterness of the novel with hope for the future. In the novel, the young girl who helps in the shop, Christine, has her hopes raised by Florence but then is crushed by the results of the eleven-plus exams. In the novel, she abandons the shop and Florence. In the film, she waves farewell to Florence as the bookseller leaves across the sunny waters of the bay; a soft fade reveals that, when she grows up, Christine follows in Florence's path and opens her own bookshop, finally fulfilling Florence's legacy. Fitzgerald does not offer this romantic fantasy. Florence's bookshop allowed her to pretend 'for a while that human beings are not divided into exterminators and exterminatees, with the former, at any given moment, predominating' (Fitzgerald 1978, 37). The novel's final sentence, as Florence leaves the town of Hardborough, is among the most heart-breaking in literature.

The connection between hope and bookstores provided in the film version of *The Bookshop* is offered in many of the novels. The bookstore is a haven, a place where people are safe. As Jean Perdue, the self-styled literary apothecary in *The Little Paris Bookshop*, notes: '[I]t was a common misconception that booksellers looked after books. They looked after people' (George 2015, 22). Perdue sells books to heal peoples lives. He describes a book as 'both a medic and medicine at once. It makes a diagnosis as well as offering therapy. Putting the right novels to the appropriate ailments: that's how I sell books' (George 2015, 27).

It is a message echoed by Oren Teicher of the ABA: '[P]utting the right book in a person's hand at the right moment can change a life' (Teicher 2012). To do this requires an ability by the bookseller to know the literature that is available to the reader, empathize with the person and make the appropriate connection. At the opening of *The Little Paris Bookshop*, Perdue refuses to sell to a woman the novel she has selected for herself, insisting instead on another that will better suit her condition:

> You need your own room. Not too bright, with a kitten to
> keep you company. And this book, which you will please
> read slowly, so you can take the occasional break. You'll do
> a lot of thinking and probably a bit of crying. For yourself.
> For the years. (George 2015, 13)

Rather than object to the patronizing tone, the woman takes the book. She returns later, happier, demanding more of the same.

Perdue himself flees his life in Paris when he discovers a tragic truth from his past. He departs on his book barge, travelling the canals of France on a journey of discovery that he navigates with the insights of his books. The voyage is both toward the truth of lost love and away from the new love he has left in Paris. On the barge, meeting other readers and writers, he learns that he can love the woman he left in Paris. This love develops in the bookshop, not in the company of the beloved; the books, their truths and the conversations they inspire with friends provide the insight he needs to find love.

Perdue flourishes because he brought his bookshop to the world; A.J. Fikry, the owner of Island Books ('approximately $350,000 per annum in sales, the better portion of that in the summer months to folks on holiday' (Zevin 2014, 5)), flourishes only when the external world invades his bookstore. Fikry is grieving over the recent death of his wife in a car accident. He lives above his store, drowning his sorrows on bad wine and Indian take-aways. He reaches a new low when he drunkenly leaves his most valued possession, a rare first edition of

Poe's *Tamerlane*, on the kitchen table overnight and it is stolen. Then a baby girl (Maya) is left on his doorstep. To care for it, he is forced to engage with the local community and his wife's family. He discovers the courage to leave the island to seek romance with a publishers rep. He encourages the local police officer to start a book club. In the end, he grows ill and dies, leaving behind a wife, a daughter, friends and a thriving bookstore.

The title of this history is *The Collected Works of A.J. Fikry*. It is structured around a list of short stories he recommends to Maya, now his adopted daughter, each story a comment on his own life as it reawakens. In the end, as he lies dying, he thinks of what he wants to tell her: 'We are not quite novels. The analogy he is looking for is almost there. We are not quite short stories. At this point, his life is seeming closest to that. In the end, we are collected works' (Zevin 2014, 236).

His collected works include the story of his wife, the story of his daughter, the stories of his friends and his community. If, as Casey argues 'places gather' (Casey 1996), then this bookstore gathers people through the power of the books and stories that define the space. For the infant Maya, who was abandoned on the steps, the store is the whole world:

> There are sixteen stairs until you get to the bookstore. Maya slides her bottom down each one because her legs are too short to manage the flight with confidence. She toddles across the store, past the books that don't have pictures in them, past the greeting cards. She runs her hand across the magazines, gives the rotating stand with the bookmarks a spin. Good morning, magazines! Good morning, bookmarks! Good morning, books! Good morning, store! (Zevin 2014, 77)

Anyone who has been a small child in a bookstore might empathize with this vision of a world of books meant for your pleasure (if not for reading). When the bookseller dies, the people of the town worry about what will become of the store:

It matters who placed *A Wrinkle in Time* in your twelve-year
-old daughter's nail-bitten fingers or who sold you that *Let's
Go* travel guide to Hawaii or who insisted that your aunt
with the very particular tastes would surely adore *Cloud
Atlas*. Furthermore, they like Island Books. And even
though they aren't always perfectly faithful, even though
they buy e-books sometimes and shop online, they like what
it says about their town that Island Books is right in the
centre of the main strip, that it's the second or third place
you come to after you get off the ferry. (Zevin 2014, 237–8)

The bookstore created by A.J. Fikry enacts cultural, commercial and
personal meanings. The books matter as markers of the lives of the people,
providing physical representations of the giving, receiving and reading of
objects that bind people together with common understanding. But equally
important is the way the store enhances the community. A quality bookstore in the centre of the town attracts tourists and raises property values. It
also provides a landscape that a small child can explore.

Bookstores as complexes of commerce and ideas provide a natural
intersection point for various lives. Frequently the book and the life
become interchangeable, as in the *Codex Vitae* of Aldus Manutius in *Mr
Penumbra's 24-Hour Bookstore*. The readers in this San Francisco store do
not browse; instead they seek to unlock a centuries-old mystery of eternal
life. They spend their days working to decode the *Codex Vitae* of the
fifteenth-century Venetian publisher and printer Aldus Manutius, his
autobiography encoded with a cypher that has never been solved. The
readers at Mr Penumbra's believe the printer discovered a way to encode
his life within a book and they encode their own lives in books that are
stored on the shelves, believing that, once the code is decrypted, Aldus
will live again and they will share eternal life. Once again, the books that
are stored in the bookstore (like those in the Cemetery of Forgotten
Books) wait for their resurrection.

In *The Secret of Lost Things* (Hay 2010), the protagonist, Rosemary
Savage, blends the lives in the books with the lives of the staff and the
customers in the Arcade Bookstore where she works. She brings them

together in a romantic fantasy of the store as a modern-day Pequod: 'The Arcade is like the ship to me. You know, people from everywhere, on a great adventure' (Hay 2010, 139). The connection between lives lived and books stored on shelves is manifest from her first encounter with the store:

> The Arcade was population, mass, was the accomplishment of a city. Books were stacked like the teeming New Yorkers, invisible inside their buildings, but sensed as bees in a hive. The hum of life issuing from the crowds that filled the city I had begun to experience, but in the Arcade that buzzing life was made calculable in things. Chaps always told Mother and me books were minds on the shelf. Here it was true: books didn't seem inanimate; a kind of life rose from the piles heaped on tables before me. (Hay 2010, 25–6)

This is the romantic vision of a young person who has recently lost her family and had to leave her home in Tasmania to live in New York. Like Fikry, she sees people as 'collected works', the literature on the shelves reflecting and amplifying the characters of the staff and the customers.

Despite the variety of characters working in the Arcade, the store is owned and controlled by Mr Pike, a bookseller in the gruff, knowledgeable mould of Roger Mifflin. He spends his days behind the counter pricing volumes for sale or ordering the staff around like a martinet. The manager is the albino Walter Geist who rules the basement floors, while the top of the building is operated by the pipe-smoking Robert Mitchell. The Arcade Bookstore (like the Owl and Lost For Words) is a space created and controlled by men. Esme, Loveday and Rosemary all seek haven from male antagonists within the safety of male bookstores; Rosemary is among the few who find peril within their chosen haven as she becomes caught up in the internal power struggles. In contrast, the entrepreneurial havens created by Nina, Hannah and Sara are small, independent and operated by the women who establish them. Although each of these bookseller heroines finds romance in the arms of a man, they each meet their man on equal footing. The men are as likely to find haven with them.

These novels define at least three fantasies of the bookstore as a haven. In one, the store is an opportunity to find freedom and to define oneself; protagonists like Nina, Hannah and Sara use their bookstores to recreate their lives. Their bookstores provide a place where they can stand and defy the world. The risks this defiance entails is evident in tales such as that of Florence Green. Defiance can require greater courage and strength than a bookseller expects, as Florence Green found to her cost.

The bookstore also provides a haven in a past world in which the wisdom in the books and their caretakers provide security for the future. The Owl, the Arcade and Lost for Words are as much museums preserving past literature as they are shops for consumption. Esme describes the Owl Bookstore as being like a museum, a place 'to keep past treasures safe through the neglect'. 'Secondhand bookshops', she explains, 'are some of the tugs that can bring the bounty safely to harbour' (Meyler 2013, 3). These are often male-dominated spaces, overseen by cantankerous but wise and good-hearted older men. The stores themselves typically specialize in used, antiquarian or rare books, preserving a past store of knowledge.

Bookstores are also havens for communities. As in *The Collected Works of A.J. Fikry*, bookstores have multiple social roles. This truth is manifested to the readers of Broken Wheel and the customers of *The Bookshop on the Corner*. Jean Perdeu's apothecarial ability to dispense the needed book to the individual customer from his book barge in Paris reflects Roger Mifflin's insight that 'People don't go to a bookseller until some serious mental accident or disease makes them aware of their danger' (Morley 1923, 9).

This communal aspect of the bookstore has led it to be included in generalizations about Oldenburg's 'third places', which 'exist on neutral ground and serve to level their guests to a condition of social equality' (1989, 42). Oldenburg described these third places as social spaces, where regulars feel welcome, the mood is often playful, and conversation is prized. However, as Laing and Royle have pointed out in their study of chain bookstores browsers in a bookstore rarely converse; browsing is seen by many to be an intensely personal experience rather than a social one (Laing and Royle 2013). In these novels, the space of the bookstore is not a 'third place' in Oldenburg's model, yet it provides the same 'sense of wholeness and distinctiveness' (Oldenburg and Brissett 1982, 265).

They often (although not always) provide 'neutral ground' where anyone is free to enter and browse. As such, they provide convenient narrative hubs for bringing together a variety of characters. They also provide a counter-space between commerce and culture, creating a potential dynamic for narratives such as the detective and mystery novels explored in the next section.

Bibliomysteries

Bibliomysteries as a genre dominate the bibliography of bookstore novels. More than 290 of the books listed can be tagged with Otto Penzler's definition of the genre: 'mystery story that involves the world of books: a bookshop, a rare volume, a library, a collector, or a bookseller'. All but nine of the forty-seven series included in the bibliography involve a main character who works in a bookstore and solves mysteries (usually murder mysteries). Bookstores appear to be a place where people frequently die, but perhaps, more importantly, also a place where mysteries are solved.

Corpses are regularly found in novel bookstores. Most are shot or stabbed, but some are killed by bookshelves. The Haven't Got a Clue bookstore in Stoneham, New Hampshire is in an especially dangerous location for bibliophiles; in the course of fifteen volumes, corpses are found in the washroom, the cookery section, the dumpster, under a bookcase, out back and out front. The small town of Pine Hills is similarly at risk from its bookstore café, Death by Coffee, in which bibliophiles are frequently found dead. And the owner of Death on Demand solves twenty-seven mysteries over a period lasting thirty years.

The bookstore as a murder setting typically confounds those investigating. Sergeant Wigan, in *Death of a Bookseller*, like many others, believes a bookstore to be a safe place, a haven of scholarship and good company. The death of his friend the bookseller is equally shocking to him because it was a friend and because he was a bookseller in a bookstore. The Milanese Inspector De Vincenzi, a popular fictional detective in Italy in the 1930s, finds it difficult to believe when told that a corpse has been found in a bookstore in *Death in a Bookstore* (*Sei donne e un libro*). 'At eight o'clock this morning, the corpse of Senator Magni was found in a bookshop in Via

Corridoni. A murder. But not a vulgar murder, not a crime for money' (De Angelis and Sinclair 1936, chap. 1).

The pattern for bibliomysteries was established in some of the earliest versions. *The Colfax Book-Plate* was first published in 1926 and serialized between June and November 1928. The story is set in the fictional Darrow's New and Secondhand Bookshop on Fourth Avenue, part of New York's bookseller's row. The plot revolves around a rare medical book that links two feuding families. The events of the story are confined mostly to the shop itself, narrated by Constance Fuller who works as a book indexer and watches the events unfold while working diligently on the next book catalogue. She is not a detective; an actual police detective is brought in for that purpose. While she and the other staff of the store misunderstand most of what happens, it is their knowledge of book history and book plates that provides the key with which the professional solves the case.

In the 1936 novel *Death in a Bookstore*, Inspector de Vincenzi finds it difficult to conceive of a murder in a place with 'too many books. The rooms, with their dim, swampy light, smelled of dust' (De Angelis and Sinclair 1936, chap. 2). The murder this time involves a missing book and a corpse in a locked room. The original Italian title of the book, *Sei donne e un libro*, translates as Six Women and a Book and indicates the importance of the people who are connected by the bookstore, its owners, employers and customers. The bookstore works well as a site for murder mysteries as it combines culture with commerce and thereby attracts suspects from many walks of life.

Bernard J. Farmer, author of *The Gentle Art of Book Collecting* wrote the less gentle *Death of a Bookseller* in 1956. Once again it is the professionals who solve the case. Police Sergeant Wigan befriends a bookseller who teaches him the art of bibliography. When the bookseller is murdered, it is Wigan who realizes that the murderer comes from the cutthroat world of rare book dealing. The detective bibliophile would reappear several times when the bibliomystery genre became popular later in the century.

These early bibliomysteries establish the antiquarian book dealing as an exotic landscape built on arcane bodies of knowledge. Inspector de Vincenzi is right to be surprised that a body has been found in a bookstore, a space of knowledge, tradition, culture – a haven for the past. The bookstore in these tales, however, is also a space of commerce where items of rare value are traded. These bibliomysteries establish the bookstore as a space where knowledge, culture and greed naturally intersect.

More than 260 of the bibliomysteries in the bibliography belong to series set in bookstores. This number excludes several that are part of detective series that does not normally involve bookstores, such as the Italian detective Inspector de Vincenzi. The first of the Hugo Marston crime novels, for instance, is *The Bookseller*. Marston is a security officer in Paris who notices when one of the *bouquinistes* on the Seine disappears. His passion for books continues to define his character throughout the series, however *The Bookseller* remains the only case directly involving booksellers.

Wayne Warga's detective and book dealer Jeffery Dean in *Hardcover* was the first post-war bookseller to be the central character in a series of novels. He discovers a forged Steinbeck autograph on a copy of *Sweet Thursday* and, using this and his connections with the CIA, uncovers and foils a terrorist plot to kill the president. Dean would appear in two more novels, but neither would achieve the success of *Hardcover*. Both maintained slight connections with the book world, using bookselling to bring Dean onto a case.

Bibliomystery series have evolved to include a bookstore specializing in mystery novels and a bookseller who applies his or her genre knowledge to solving murders that happen with unusual frequency. Books in these mystery series are united by a common central location or profession and a group of characters whose relationships develop through each new volume, creating a continuous storyline. A bookstore that specializes in mystery or crime novels is a natural home location for these series, as evidenced by the bookstores owned by Adrien English (the Cloak and Dagger Bookstore), Krissy Hancock (the Death by Coffee Bookstore), Tricia Miles (the Haven't Got a Clue Bookstore), Kati Hirschel ('Istanbul's only mystery bookshop') and Penelope Thornton-McClure (the Buy the Book bookstore).

Frequently these stores function simply as an explanation for why the protagonist can solve the mystery. As Kati Hirschel explains in *Hotel Bosphorus*, the first in a series of mystery novels set in Istanbul: 'I'd been reading crime fiction since my childhood, and selling it for the last three years. I was no longer just an ordinary reader. The time had come for me to offer my theoretical knowledge for the benefit of society' (Aykol 2011, chap. 2). The stores also function as an intersection point for the lives of many people. The first victim in the Haunted Bookshop Mysteries, *The Ghost and Mrs McLure*, is a popular writer who has come to do a reading in the store. The Bookstore Cafe Mysteries begin literally with *Death by Coffee* in the store's coffee shop; in subsequent novels, the murders involve book clubs, literary agents and local censors (all the deaths in the series are somehow connected to hot drinks). Barrett's Booktown Mysteries do not focus on the single shop. Instead, the murders are committed in or around the variety of bookstores in the fictional book town of Stoneham.

In each of those series, the bookstore functions primarily as a meeting place and source of expertise in crime solving. In contrast, the bookstores owned by Dido Hoare and Cliff Janeway are important as places where antiquarian book knowledge resides. For antiquarian dealers Hoare and Janeway, visitors are customers rather than members of a local community. Hoare's story as it evolves through the series of books is as much about surviving as an independent bookseller in London as it is building a community. The continuing characters include her father (a researcher) and her young son. The crimes committed generally revolve around rare manuscripts or books; the victims are customers. In *Die Once* (2003), for instance, Hoare investigates the murder of a regular customer because his cheque bounced and she needs to retrieve the book. The MacGuffin in the first mystery in the series, 1996 *Death's Autograph*, is a possible Shakespeare signature, followed by an Egyptian codex (*Ghost Walk*) and a book estate (*Smoke Screen*). By the fourth volume, *Road Kill*, the narrative focus has shifted from antiquarian books to Hoare's personal life, with nanny problems and customer conflicts replacing rare manuscripts as the problem to be solved.

Cliff Janeway's adventures evolve similarly, from books as objects of desire and value to books as clues to a mystery. When Janeway is first introduced in *Booked to Die*, he is a homicide detective in Denver, Colorado with a passion for collecting rare books. The plot involves the murder of a book scout. Midway through the story, he leaves the force and opens a store, Twice Told Books. When he eventually solves the book scout's murder, it is only partly due to his bibliographic knowledge. More important is his knowledge and understanding of the local book trade. He knows all the book dealers from having been a customer and later from being a member of the trade. And he understands their passion for books. The murder is solved because he recognizes how a book dealer loses track of time when absorbed in bibliographic work.

The novel is filled with bibliographic details. He even describes his lover in terms of her bibliographic knowledge:

> She still doesn't understand the first edition game: Hemingway, she says, reads just as well in a two-bit paperback as he does in a $500 first printing. I can still hear myself lecturing her the first time she said that. Only a fool would read a first edition. (Dunning 1992, 6)

That knowledge is put in perspective when he speaks to book dealers, who respect his knowledge but recognize that his perspective is that of a collector, not a bookseller. Equally important to the murder case is knowledge of the book world and Dunning provides a complex picture of that world in 1986, the year in which the novel is set. In his foreword to the 2000 edition, he laments some of the changes to the world he describes, such as the role of the book scout:

> He's a guy who can't make it in the real world. He operates out of the trunk of a car, if he's lucky enough to have a car, out of a knapsack or a bike bag if he isn't. He's an outcast, a fighter, or a man who's been driven out of every other line of work. He can be quiet and humble or aggressive and intimidating. Some are renegades and, yes, there are a few psychos. The one thing the best of them have in common is an eye for books. It's almost spooky, a pessimistic book dealer once said – the nearest thing you can think of to prove the existence of God. How these guys, largely uneducated, many unread, gravitate toward books and inevitably choose the good ones is a prime mystery of human nature.
>
> (Dunning 1992, i)

Dunning himself is the owner of a second-hand bookstore in Denver (the setting for his novels) and that experience especially informs the second half of the novel, in which Janeway quits the police force to open a second-hand store. He receives several lessons from other book dealers in the city, many of whom see another bookstore as an asset for book-selling rather than just another competitor. It is here, from his base in his store, that he is finally able to unite his detective skills with his biblio-graphic interests to solve the murder. The murder itself is revealed as having been planned around the bookman's passion for the book as an object of desire and obsession.

The second book in the series, *The Bookman's Wake* (1995), continues his bibliographic crime solving. His shop this time provides only the initial location for the start of the adventure when a former cop comes to ask his assistance in a murder involving books. The action then moves from Denver to Seattle where his expertise in book provenance and production allow him to solve the murder. In this novel, the bookstore is an interesting location for the first meeting with a villain and quickly provides a background for the protagonist. Books, their value, provenance and production remain the key to the solution of the murder. In the third volume, *The Bookman's Promise* (2004), bookselling moves even further away from the centre and the books themselves are reduced to objects that initiate the action but are unimportant in themselves.

The longest running series of bibliomysteries are the Death on Demand books by Caroline Hart. The series starts in 1987, when one of the most popular television series of the time, *Murder She Wrote* starring Angela Lansbury, was in its fourth season at CBS. Hart's series would include many of the same elements as the television series: a small coastal town, a female protagonist with an interest in mystery novels, a collection of local char-acters and the friendship of a local sheriff. The novels owe an equal debt to the Thin Man novels and the style offered by Page in *Fast Company*. Hart describes the novel as 'an old-fashioned mystery, a light-hearted, fun, good-humoured book without an ounce of angst' (Hart 2005, 45). Much of this is provided by the light-hearted repartee between Annie Laurence, owner of the Death on Demand mystery bookstore and her friend (and eventual husband), wealthy detective Max Darling.

The series begins with a classic mystery scenario. A group of mystery writers are in the bookstore listening to a man who is threatening to blackmail each of them. Suddenly the lights go out and when Annie gets them back on, the man is lying dead on the floor. The mystery writers in the room quickly start to assess the plot:

> Harriet enthusiastically moved from the general to the particular. 'A classic locked-room situation. He's standing in front of a room facing –' she counted '– eleven people, the lights go out, presto, he's dead. The murderer has to be one of the eleven.' (Hart 1987, chap. 6)

Annie is the prime suspect, but everyone there had a motive for the murder. Annie, joined by Max, uses her knowledge of murder mystery plots, motives and characters to solve the case, all the while verballing sparring with Max and resisting his romantic suggestions.

The series would continue for thirty years and twenty-seven volumes, mostly set on the small island of Broward Rock where her store is located. Victims are supplied by customers, authors with tell-all books and the tourists who regularly visit the town. The plots are tightly woven and make liberal use of classic mystery novel tropes and references. Jessica Fletcher in *Murder She Wrote* solved the frequent murders in Cabot Cove (and anywhere else she might travel to) with her expertise as a crime novelist. Annie achieves the same results through her expertise as a seller of mystery books.

Frequently in bibliomysteries, the solution to the crime depends on either bibliographic knowledge or experience of the rare book trade. However, in *Midnight at the Bright Ideas Bookstore* the solution to the mystery is encrypted directly into books bought in the store. A homeless man, Joey, hangs himself one night at the Bright Ideas Bookstore. The store clerk, Lydia, who had befriended him at the store, discovers he has encrypted messages to her in the books. He cuts holes in the pages of one book so that, when the page is placed over the same page in another, the words that are revealed form cryptic sentences. 'No one waited outside the gates … I was released … free' (Sullivan 2017, 117). The decryption depends on Lydia's recognizing the store's book labelling system, so she knows which books Joey used as pairs.

The idea of books as puzzles to be solved to reveal a great treasure informs the bibliomysteries of Charlie Lovett, *The Bookman's Tale: A Story of Obsession* (2013) and *First Impressions* (2014). Both mysteries begin with a book that leads the protagonist to discoveries in literary history. In *The Bookman's Tale*, the discovery is an old oil colour portrait pressed between the pages of a book. The hero's obsession with the painting (which impossibly appears to be that of his recently deceased wife) leads him to discover truths about William Shakespeare. *First Impressions* begins with a search for a copy of the rare second edition of *Little Book of Allegories* by Richard Mansfield. A close study of that text may reveal that Jane Austen plagiarized *Pride and Prejudice*. The truth can only be discovered through a careful bibliographic study of the manuscripts involved; the importance of the answer is evidenced by a murder.

Neither of the two women who run the Biblio Bookstore in Chennai, India, is a detective; both are, however, bibliographic experts. They locate, appraise, price and sell books – antiquarian and otherwise. They are both held in esteem within the Indian rare book community for their knowledge and experience. Their story, as told in *The Book Hunters of Katpadi* (2017), involves both crime (the uncovering of a scam involving a rare book collection) and a bibliographic hunt to uncover a literary secret, an unknown volume by Sir Richard Francis Burton. Their methods are purely bibliographic. They follow the clues provided by the books they find, carefully researching their history and provenances.

Entire chapters of *Katpadi* are dedicated to discussions of such arcana as the best biographies of Burton or the current techniques for small book printing. The section on bibliomysteries contributed valuable bibliographic material for the current book. The novel uses the concept of bibliomystery to explore the rich antiquarian book culture of India. Its author, Pradeep Sebastian, is an Indian journalist who writes on book culture. He has also produced a collection of essays on bibliophilia, *The Groaning Shelf*.

Every mystery story has a crime, victim and motive. In *A Novel Bookstore* (*Au bon roman*) (2012) by the French journalist Laurence

Cossé, the crime is not against any individual or even a group; it is against a Parisian bookstore and the concept that drives that store. The owners, former comic-book salesman Ivan and wealthy heiress Francesca, meet by chance, discover a common passion for good literature and develop a plan for their ideal bookstore. Theirs will not be an ordinary bookstore for ordinary customers. Their store will stock only 'good' novels, ones that are more literary than commercial – books that Francesca describes as 'necessary books, books we can read the day after a funeral, when we have no tears left from all our crying':

> We want books that cost their authors a great deal, books where you can feel the yers of work, the backache, the writer's block, the author's panic at the thought that he might be lost: his discouragement, his courage, his anguish, his stubbornness, the risk of failure that he has taken.
>
> (Cossé 2012, 278–9)

The mystery that drives the plot of *The Novel Bookstore* is what motive anyone would have for trying to destroy such a bookstore. It is a mystery that goes directly to the question of a bookstore's purpose in society. What social, cultural or commercial functions does a bookstore fulfil?

Francesca has a fortune to spend; Ivan has experience of bookselling. Together, they open the Good Novel Bookstore on the rue Dupuytren, the same street on which Sylvia Beach first opened Shakespeare and Company in 1919. They develop a detailed business plan that includes marketing, location, staffing and other business details. One reviewer of the novel described it as 'more like a business plan than a page-turner' (Hand 2010).

They also develop a complex system for choosing the stock of 'good novels', which involves identifying six committee members with suitable literary tastes and asking each to contribute 600 titles of books they consider 'good'. The members of this committee are kept anonymous through an elaborate scheme and they are not even known to one another. The Good Novel Store is funded by Francisca with a grand opening that is a success and it makes a splash in the Parisian press.

The shop's success brings it enemies. Ivan and Francesca must turn to a police detective when three of their committee members are attacked. Soon newspaper articles and advertisements start to attack the store as elitist. Someone funds the opening of several other bookstores on the same street, stores with names like The Pleasurable Novel and The Excellent Novel but that sell books merely because they are popular or recent releases. The Good Novel concept has raised the concerns of the publishing industry and of mediocre novelists whose work does not appear in the Good Novel Bookstore.

No one is murdered – there is only one suicide. And bibliographic investigation provides no clues. Neither does any detective or book-seller make use of genre knowledge to solve the crimes; there is no mystery bookstore, just the mystery. The police detective works tire-lessly in the background, providing vague updates on the investigation to the two booksellers but never uncovering solid evidence. An attempt to get the courts involved fails for want of criminal evidence. No conclusion is ever reached. The attacks may have been organized by the publishing houses or disgruntled authors; it may have been a movement or a conspiracy. Whatever the exact nature of the attacks, the detective is sure of their importance; he reports that 'something happened here that is comparable to what happened with Al Qaeda and its consequences' (Cossé 2012, 386).

The battle over the bookstore takes place mostly in the media and the commercial spaces of Paris. Both sides publish defences of their vision for literature in the papers. Both sides open bookstores that reflect their vision. Both sides benefit from the attention their battle brings to book-selling, not to mention the value of having a street in Paris that becomes famous for its bookstores. The Good Novel Bookstore believes in quality writing and makes little distinction between popular or elitist literature, as a supporter explains:

> You cannot oppose popular literature and elitist literature,
> that there is in fact no point in trying to distinguish them,
> never mind the fact that it can be difficult. Both types of
> literature include a number of insignificant books and a few

masterpieces, and the only worthwhile distinction is to
promote great books, some of which are very simple while
others are difficult. (Cossé 2012, 243)

The publishing houses and writers who make a living from their storytelling
insist that the bookstore's elitist attitude discriminates against what most
people want in their fiction and what the publishers need to be able to
provide to survive commercially. By opening the Good Novel Bookstore,
Ivan and Francesca have rebelled against that ethos. Like every independent
bookstore, they have had to establish an independent identity. They have
stood out from the crowd. The other stores that open on the Rue Dupuytren
are owned by anonymous 'investors', apparently corporate-run shops. Only
The Good Novel is an independent store and as such its success would be an
industry disruptor.

In the end, the store survives only because it downsizes and moves away
from the centre of Paris. When the finances are examined closely, it
becomes clear that it was never a commercial success, with its costs out-
matching its sales. (There are echoes here of Amazon's famous first decade
in business when it regularly ran at a loss as it disrupted the industry.) In its
smaller state, its impact grows. New, independent 'Good Novel' stores
begin to open around the world, inspired by Ivan and Francesca's operation.
It achieves online success by selling its stock online. Like other independents, its success is founded on curation that reflects the owner's passions
and that business model is replicable.

Mr Penumbra's 24-Hour Bookstore, in contrast, has a business model that
cannot be replicated. By the end of Robin Sloan's 2012 novel, the store has
been replaced by a climbing wall. Forty years before, it had been a vibrant
bookstore full of young San Franciscans experiencing the freedoms of the
1960s. When the story opens, the customers have all but disappeared and the
store's owner, Mr Ajax Penumbra, makes no effort to sell what stock of new
books it does have. Instead, the store has become a sort of lending library
for members of a cult who are working to solve a 500-year-old mystery and
achieve eternal life.

The visitors to the shop are working to decode the *Codex Vitae* of Aldus
Manutius – founder of the Aldine Press in 1494, inventor of italic type and

designer of many of the finest books ever produced. The visitors are members of the Unbroken Spine, an international cult whose members believe that Manutius discovered the secret of eternal life. This secret was encrypted in his *Codex Vitae* and the key given to his friend, Griffo Gerriszoon (a character loosely based on Francesco Griffo, the Italian punchcutter who created the fonts for Manutius). Members of the cult encode their own lives into individual *codices vitae*, which are stored in a library in New York, a sort of typographic cryogenics chamber. It is believed that, once the Unbroken Spine manages to decode the Manutius *Codex*, 'every member of the Unbroken Spine who ever lived . . . will live again'. (Sloan 2012, 136).

When unemployed graphics designer Clay Jansson takes the night shift at Penumbra's bookstore, he brings with him a friend who works as a data visualizer at Google and together they realize that a computer can decode these texts more efficiently than human scholars. The books themselves appear to be nothing but 'a solid matrix of letters, a blanket of glyphs with hardly a trace of white space. The letters are big and bold, punched onto the paper in a sharp serif. . . . The pages are just long runs of letters – an undifferentiated jumble' (Sloan 2012, 29). Scanning the Manutius Codex and running the text through an algorithm, applying the vast might of the Google computer system, reveals that there is no message, no pattern to the letters. It is all noise.

Mr Penumbra's store has stood for nearly a century, storing the codices of its members as they work through the patterns of letters. The physical layout of the store is taller than it is wide. A prequel written shortly after *Mr Penumbra* explains that its design was based on a ship that was buried under San Francisco during the Gold Rush days. The codices are kept in the upper reaches, three floors up, accessed by tall ladders. Later, Clay will realize that his favourite book, a fantasy novel, was based on the bookstore: 'The tower reaches up to the stars, and each floor has its own set of rules, its puzzles to solve' (2012, 263). The air of mystery, grandeur and fantasy that the layout gives to the books is what attracts Clay to the store.

The Google campus, which Clay visits with his girlfriend the data visualizer, presents a sharp contrast to the physical bookstore. It is brightly lit and full of engaged, interesting people. And it contains vast amounts of data, which the Googlers describe as knowledge. No physical space could contain it all. 'Everything at Google runs in the Big Box':

> She points a brown arm toward a container with www stencilled across the side in tall green letters. 'There's a copy of the web in there.' YT: 'Every video on YouTube.' MX: 'All your email. Everybody's email.'
>
> Penumbra's shelves don't seem so tall anymore. (2012, 83)

Clay also surrounds himself with people grounded in the material world. His co-worker at the bookstore (day-shift) is an archaeologist ('I don't really mess with anything newer than the twelfth century' (2012, 109). His roommate works for the special effects company Industrial Light and Magic but spends his free time building 'Matropolis', a cityscape built from 'boxes and cans, paper and foam' (2012, 23). Clay himself is a creative, working digitally with fonts and graphic design. Bringing the digital world into the bookstore resulted in failure; Google's decoding of the *Codex* resulted in only noise and the apparent repudiation of five centuries of bibliographic scholarship. When Clay starts to think of the codices as material objects, however, he succeeds in understanding Aldus Manutius' intentions.

He realizes that the key to the mystery is the fonts themselves, created by Griffo Gerriszoon 500 years earlier to encode his friend's life story. When he finds and examines the font punches themselves, he discovers the key to the encryption engraved on them. The truth, he points out in the epilogue, is 'built on friendship and work done with care. All the secrets worth knowing are hiding in plain sight' (2012, 288). He solves the mystery while listening to a recording of his favourite book, although he had to buy a Walkman in an antiques store to do so. He ends the novel working with Mr Penumbra as a consultant working with 'companies operating at the intersection of books and technology, trying to solve the mysteries that gather in the shadows of digital shelves' (2012, 285) – starting with Google and their new e-reader.

Having solved the mystery, the novel ends in a contradiction. Despite the material artefact having proved its value, the twenty-four-hour bookstore is abandoned and becomes a climbing wall. Manutius' *Codex Vitae* is decoded at

Google and published on Google Books, one more item in the Big Box. The mystery that drove 500 years of scholarship has proved to be false hope, the cryogenic chamber is merely a place to hide lives lived. This bookstore no longer has a function in the digital age; computer algorithms and digital texts are better options for decoding patterns of knowledge. Even the material objects, Griffo Gerriszoon's punches, are digitized to allow the font to be used and the codices to be decoded. Material objects are of interest only to archaeologists and artists. Mr Penumbra realizes that early in the novel. He mentions to Clay that he thought young people today read everything on their mobile phones, to which Clay responds that many people still like the smell of books. 'The smell!' Penumbra repeats. 'You know you are finished when people start talking about the smell' (Sloan 2012, 65).

4 The Fantasy of the Bookstore

Christopher Morley's two early bookstore novels, *Parnassus on Wheels* and *The Haunted Bookshop*, established the archetype of the independent bookstore in literature. The owner was generally male, was well-versed in bibliography and passionate about the value of books for society. The bookstore itself specialized in used and antiquarian books. Fictional bookstores that sold new books sourced directly from the publishers were scarce until the end of the century, although they flourished with the rise of the bibliomystery series. Morley's novels also established two other tropes that would define the bookstore in future literature. Helen McGill, the narrator of the first volume and a minor character in the second, was the first of the many women who would seek meaning, independence or sanctuary in a bookstore. And *The Haunted Bookshop* would be the first in a long line of mysteries with bibliography and bibliophilia at their core.

The bookstore novel has encompassed many genres, including the book industry satires of *The Nijmegan Proof* (1988) by the London bookseller Arthur Freeman and Ian Norrie's *Brought to Book* (2002); erotica such as Charlotte Stein's *Control* (2015); children's and young adults books including Cylin Busby's *The Bookstore Cat* (2020) or Peggy Christian's *The Bookstore Mouse* (2002); romances that include *Twenty-One Truths about Love* (2019) by Matthew Dicks or Annie Darling's Lonely Hearts Bookshop (2016–2018) series. In spite of this variety, bibliomystery has dominated the bookstore novel. It provides the theme for the thirty-eight of the bookstore novel series identified in the Appendix: Book Series and 286 of the novels in the bibliography (see the online Appendix: Bibliography of Bookstore Novels). Although not all bibliomysteries have involved murder, in each the bookstore acts as a place of mystery or danger. The bookstore's complex mix of commerce, culture and community brings together the characters (booksellers, collectors, authors, browsers), the motives, the means and the opportunities.

Another fantasy that has run through the novels since 1917 is the bookstore as an opportunity for (mainly) women to take control of their own lives or to find sanctuary from the outside world. Helen McGill is thrilled to take control of her own story in *Parnassus on Wheels*. Florence

Green wants 'to make it clear to herself, and possibly to others, that she existed in her own right' (Fitzgerald 1978, 2). Francisca, wife of a crass businessman and mother to a daughter who took her own life, exclaims to her new business partner: 'I too want to do something worthwhile in my life at last' (Cossé 2012, 108). Hanna (*Bookshop of the Broken Hearted*), Nina (*Bookshop on the Corner*), Shirley (*Shirley: Young Bookseller*) and Sara (*The Readers of Broken Wheel Recommend*) have all suffered in lives that were out of their control. For each one, opening a bookstore is an act of defiance in which they take a stand and start to write their own story.

The bookstore in these novels is a place of contradiction, providing both sanctuary and peril. The bookstore is a place where you can save yourself and a place where you risk your life or well being. In *Havana Fever*, Condé is confounded by the problem that only by selling the heritage of Cuba can he save the heritage of Cuba. In Hoffman's 'Escapes" the bookstore where Sylvia finds a haven and kindness is the same store that sends her abuser to a future of torture. There is tremendous power in these stores and that power is seldom understood by those who own or work in them. As both Florence and Francesco discover to their cost, that power is a threat to many.

Most of the bookstores in these novels succeed; the owners find a way to balance the contradiction inherent in their business. Yes, people frequently die in the bibliomystery series – but the community continues and in the bibliomystery series it is the bookstore that provides the continuity for the community. Francesca attempted to maintain the Good Novel bookstore with her fortune, purchasing a prime location, paying for full-page advertisements, paying the staff salaries. When the business is met with anger and resentment, when its supporters are attacked and the store mocked as elitist, when her attempts to clearly state the convictions that inform the store are met without understanding, she takes her own life. Her partner Ivan, in contrast, has been a practical worker in the store, curating stock, making it work, assuming little, pleased when he succeeds but not overwhelmed by failures, and he survives the failure of the store. He manages to reinvent it in another, less ostentatious part of Paris, makes use of internet connections to encourage similar stores in other countries and finally marries the woman he loves. Although both Ivan and Francesca care passionately about literature and novels, it is Ivan who abides in the bookstore and allows himself to be bound by the contradiction it represents. He manages to adapt his good novel locale to the Parisian commercial location.

As Ivan and Francesca's story illustrates, the bookstore is a space of tension created by competing demands. The books in the store may be literature, may be filled with profound truths, but they are equally commodities that can be sold. Those who run mystery bookstores use them to attract customers and friends and they use them to solve the murders of those customers and friends. For Nina and Jean Perdue (*The Little Paris Bookstore*), they are tools of the trade as they make a living prescribing the right book to the right person. For Cliff Janeway (*Booked to Die*) and Sergeant Wigan (*Death of a Bookseller*), they are valuable objects that a person might kill for. For Mrs Gamart (*The Bookshop*), they are an affront to her social standing, filled with ideas she cannot control. George Pike, the owner of the Arcade Bookstore in New York (*The Secret of Lost Things*), sees them as valuable commodities that need to be recorded and shelved in an orderly manner.

Within the bookstores, it is often contradictory assumptions about what a book is that create the potential for action within the space of the store, which give the space its meaning. Outside the walls of the bookstore, the locale creates its own tensions. The bookstore is part of a community, a social one, a literary one, a business one. As such, the bookstore cannot avoid interacting with the members of these communities, sometimes in concert and often in opposition. Roger Mifflin and Helen McGill take their books on the road, stirring up trouble as they go. Francesca and Ivan take their books and beliefs to Paris and arouse the forces of commerce against them. These two tensions – within the place defined by the bookstore and that place within a wider temporal-spatial space – create the multiple bookstore fantasies inscribed in these bookstore novels.

Appendix: Book Series

| Theodore I. Terhune Mysteries | Bruce Graeme | 8 Entries | 1941–1951 |

When Theodore Ichabod Terhune, bookseller and crime fiction writer, riding home on his bike one evening, saves a woman from attack by thieves. It is the start of a part-time career as an amateur detective in the small Kent village of Bray-in-the-Marsh.

| The Burglar | Lawrence Block | Twelve entries | 1977–2020 |

Bernie Rhodenbarr is the owner of Barnegat Books as well as being a professional burglar. While breaking into empty homes in New York, he frequently gets caught up in murders being committed on the premises. Bernie is regularly supported by a friendly corrupt cop.

| Jeffrey Dean Mysteries | Wayn Warga | Three entries | 1985–91 |

Jeffery Dean is a rare book dealer and ex-journalist with ties to the CIA that cause him to be caught up in international intrigues tied to the international book trade.

| Death on Demand Mysteries | Carolyn G. Hart | Twenty-seven entries | 1987–2017 |

Annie Laurence, owner of the Death on Demand bookstore specializing in mystery novels, and her partner Max Darling start to use their knowledge of murder mystery plots to solve crimes in their small island town when she becomes the prime suspect for a murder in her store.

| Cliff Janeway Mysteries | John Dunning | Five entries | 1992–2006 |

Cliff Janeway leaves the homicide department of the Denver Police in order to open an antiquarian bookstore.

| Claire Malloy Mysteries | Joan Hess | Twenty entries | 1994–2015 |

Claire Malloy, single mother and owner of the Book Depot in Farberville, Arkansas, solves the frequent murders that happen in the small town with the help of the local sheriff, with whom she develops a long-lasting relationship over the years.

| Dido Hoare Mysteries | Marianne Macdonald | Eight entries | 1996–2006 |

Dido Hoare is a single mother and antiquarian book dealer in North London. When strange deaths occur in her neighbourhood or shop, she solves the mystery with the help of her father, Barnabas, a retired Oxford professor. The mysteries normally involve books that are stolen or that provide a reason for Dido to investigate.

| Honey Huckleberry Mysteries | Margaret Moseley | Three entries | 1998–2000 |

Honey Huckleberry is a book rep travelling around the bookstores of California, encountering murders within the publishing industry.

| Cemetery of Forgotten Books | Carlos Ruiz Zafón | Four entries | 2001–18 |

Two bookstores in Barcelona, the Cemetery of Forgotten Books and Sempere and Son, provide focal points for a complex of novels set during the Spanish Civil War and in Franco's Spain.

| Poetic Death Mysteries | Diana Killian | Four entries | 2003–9 |

A schoolteacher on holiday in the Lake District becomes involved with a former jewel thief who now runs an antiques and book store, Rogues Gallery. Their romance is complicated by murders connected to works by romantic poets and by the fallout from a failed jewel heist.

| Haunted Bookshop Mysteries | Alice Kimberly | Seven entries | 2004–21 |

Recent widow and single mother Penelope Thornton-McClure runs the Buy More Books store, which is haunted by the ghost of a private detective who was murdered on its doorstep fifty years before. Together they solve unexplained deaths of authors and customers, sometimes with the help of the 'Quibble Over Anything Gang', otherwise known as the Quindicott Business Owners Association.

| Claire Gulliver Mysteries | Gayle Wigglesworth | Five entries | 2004–11 |

Claire Gulliver is a former librarian who inherited a travel bookstore from a great-uncle. Her work at the store leads her to travel the world and during these travels she meets and eventually marries a CIA agent.

| Adrien English Mysteries | Josh Lanyon | Seven entries | 2007–16 |

Adrien English is a thirty-two-year-old gay bookseller and mystery writer, owner of the Cloak and Dagger Bookstore. He begins investigating murders himself when his employee and former lover is found stabbed to death in the back alley and he becomes a suspect.

| Georgina Kincaid Series | Richelle Med | Six entries | 2007–11 |

Georgina Kincaid is a demon succubus running a bookstore in Seattle where she seduces men to claim their souls, falls in love with a mortal and becomes embroiled in demonic politics.

| Booktown Mysteries | Lorna Barrett | Fifteen entries | 2008–21 |

Stoneham, New Hampshire is the New England book town where Tricia Miles opens her mystery bookstore, Haven't Got a Clue. She starts to investigate murders with the aid of other residents of the town when the owner of a cookbook store is murdered.

| Crochet Mysteries | Betty Hechtman | Thirteen entries | 2008–21 |

Molly Pink is the event coordinator at Shedd & Royal Books and More. She organizes a the weekly crochet group in the store, but begins to investigate when the leader of the group is murdered. She takes up crocheting to catch the real killer.

| Henry Sullivan | Vincent McCaffrey | Two entries | 2009–11 |

Henry Sullivan works as a book scout in Boston, Massachusetts. His purchases from estates often place him in precarious circumstances with the law.

| Black Cat Bookstore Mysteries | Ali Brandon | Six entries | 2011–16 |

Pettistone's Fine Books, run by Darla Pettistone, is a rare books store in Brooklyn. Darla inherited the shop along with a bookstore cat, Hamlet. The cat leads its new owner into a variety of murder mysteries.

| Kati Hirschel Istanbul Mysteries | Esmahan Aykol | Three entries | 2011–15 |

Kati Hirschel owns the only mystery bookstore in Istanbul and uses her knowledge of mystery novels to investigate crimes in which her friends have become involved.

| A Raven's Nest Bookstore Mystery | Allison Kingsley | Four entries | 2011–14 |

Cousins Stephanie and Clara Quinn operate a bookstore in Maine and solve local murders using Clara's clairvoyant abilities.

| Read Wine Bookstore Cozy Mysteries | L.C. Turner | Six entries | 2012–21 |

Trixie Pristine and two friends open a bookstore and wine bar, but even before the store opens dead bodies turn up in the small town and the women need to solve crimes to save their friends and their store.

| Bookshop by the Sea | Jan Ellis | Three entries | 2013–17 |

Eleanor leaves London to open a bookstore in a quiet seaside town in Devon. Her life there becomes complicated by environmental activism, a Victorian-era murder and a complicated love life.

| Bookshop Hotel | A.K. Klemm | Three entries | 2013–17 |

A young widow returns to her home town when she inherits a hotel from her grandfather. While renovating the building, she develops it into a hotel-bookstore. The Bookshop Hotel provides a point of connection between her past and her new life.

| The Lost Bookshop | Adam Maxwell | Five entries | 2013–18 |

Two schoolchildren discover the bookstore run by their aunt and uncle has a magical backroom that transports them to other lands.

| Victorian Bookshop Mystery | Kate Parker | Five entries | 2013–17 |

Georgia Fenchurch inherits her family bookshop on the murder of her parents. Her work in the bookshop leads her to the Archivist Society, a secret society of archivists who investigate and solve murders and other crimes in Victorian London.

| Bookstore Café Mysteries | Alex Erickson | Nine entries | 2015–21 |

The daughter of a successful mystery novelist opens the Death by Coffee mystery bookstore and café. On opening day, a customer dies after drinking a coffee. Subsequent deaths include her father's agent, a local wealthy woman, Santa Claus, a wedding planner and a friend's former lover.

| The Book Lovers | Victoria Connelly | Five entries | 2015–19 |

A children's book author, Callie, moves to a small town in rural Suffolk where she becomes involved with the loves and tribulations of the Nightingale family, owners of the local used bookstore and children's bookstore.

| Highland Bookshop Mysteries | Molly MacRae | Five entries | 2016–22 |

Four women move to a small, coastal Scottish town to open a bookstore, Yon Bonnie Books. Perhaps predictably, they regularly encounter dead bodies in the shed, the tearoom, by the river and by an ancient standing stone.

| Lonely Hearts Bookshop | Annie Darling | Four entries | 2016–18 |

Posy Morland inherits Bookends, a failing bookstore she frequented as a child. She works with several friends to rebuild the store as Happy Ever After. She and her friends find romance while working at the shop.

| Magical Bookshop Mysteries | Amanda Flower | Five entries | 2016–22 |

Murder and mystery happen regularly to Violet, a former graduate student who returns to her home town in upstate New York to help her grandmother operate Charming Books, a magical bookstore.

Oxford Medieval Mysteries	Ann Swinfen	Six entries	2016–18

Nicholas Elyot is a bookseller in fourteenth-century Oxford. He and his friend, the Oxford scholar Jordain Brinkylsworth, solve crimes in the medieval town.

Scottish Bookshop Mysteries	Paige Shelton	Seven entries	2016–22

Delaney Nichols leaves Kansas to take a job as a rare book researcher at the Cracked Spine in Edinburgh, a bookshop run by the aristocratic, vastly wealthy and quite mysterious Edwin MacAlister. Her work recovering and valuing rare volumes regularly leads Delaney to involvement in murder investigations related to the books.

Paris Booksellers Cosy Mysteries	Evan Hirst	Six entries	2016

Ava Sext is a Londoner selling books from a stand overlooking the Seine. She and a fellow bookseller and notary, Henri DeAth, must solve crimes in various Parisian locations.

Camino Island	John Grisham	Two Entries	2017–20

Rare book dealer Bruce Cable operates Bay Books on Camino Island in Florida and is a suspect in various thefts of rare book manuscripts and murders.

Mystery Bookshop	V.M. Burns	Seven entries	2017–21

The owner of a mystery bookstore on the shores of Lake Michigan also writes historical cosy mysteries. The events in her novels begin to resemble events in real life and she becomes both novelist and detective.

Sherlock Holmes Bookshop Mysteries	Vicki Delany	Seven entries	2017–22

The Sherlock Holmes Bookshop and Emporium is located at 222 Baker Street in the fictional Cape Cod town of west London and sells Arthur Conan Doyle reprints and new books about the Holmes legend. When the store's half-owner, Gemma Doyle, becomes a suspect in a local murder she begins investigating.

Theodore & the Enchanted Bookstore	Kristine Kibbee and Julianne Winter	Four entries	2017–20

Theodore is a corgi that is adopted by bookstore owner Sam, who finds a pair of spectacles to help the dog navigate the store, but the spectacles are magical and lead Theodore on adventures across time in this series for young adults.

| Back Room Bookstore Cozy Mystery | Susan Harper | Four entries | 2018–19 |

Monica Montoya, her familiar (the cat Abigail) and her assistant Holly run Backroom Books, a store located on a portal between the real and magical worlds.

| Beyond the Page Bookstore Mysteries | Lauren Elliott | Six entries | 2018–21 |

Former Boston librarian Addie Greyborne inherits a mansion and library in a small New England town that shares her name. She decides to open a used bookstore, but the new business is quickly disrupted by thefts and a local murders.

| The Bookstore Series | Alice V.L. | Two entries | 2018 |

The book, *Passage of Time*, hidden in the shelves of the Fine Books rare bookstore, contains the legend of Adelaine Alandrali. Those who read the legend are sent back in time with an opportunity to repair past mistakes in their lives.

| Foyle's Bookshop Girls | Elaine Roberts | Three entries | 2018–19 |

Three childhood friends work together at Foyle's Bookshop in London during the First World War.

| St. Marin's Cozy Mysteries | A.C.F. Bookens | Nine entries | 2019–21 |

After divorcing her husband in San Francisco, Harvey Beckett moves to Maryland to open a small town bookstore in a former garage. When the body of the local, mean-spirited news reporter is found in the store's backroom on opening day (after threatening to give the store a poor review), Harvey becomes the chief suspect and must investigate.

| Curious Bookstore Cozy Mysteries | Sophie Love | Five entries | 2020–21 |

On the day that Alexis Blair loses her publishing job and breaks up with her boyfriend, she decides to leave Boston and take a job at a bookstore in a small seaside town. She finds the store and the town to be a truly magical place.

| Mysterious Ink Bookstore | Leeann Betts | Four entries | 2020–21 |

Margie Hanson and her mystery-writing grandmother travel to Colorado when Great-aunt Rosella, owner of a mystery bookstore, is found dead. Margie inherits the store and continues to solve the murders that are frequently linked to the books she sells.

| Slaughtered Lamb Bookstore | Seana Kelly | Two entries | 2020–21 |

Seven years ago, Sam Quinn was attacked, raped and forcibly turned into a werewolf. She now runs a bookstore/bar that caters to the supernatural community of San Francisco.

| Flora Steele Mysteries | Merryn Allingham | Three entries | 2021–2 |

In the 1950s, Flora Steele, long-time resident of Abbeymead in Sussex and owner of the local bookstore, discovers a body in the back of her bookstore on the same day she meets the charismatic detective J.A. Carrington. Together they work to solve this mystery and others that occur in Abbeymead.

| Amish Bookstore | Beth Wiseman | One entry | 2022 |

The series begins with a romantic triangle between an Amish bookstore owner, his Amish assistant and an outsider eager to purchase a book the owner has promised not to sell.

References

Agnew, John A. 2014. *Place and Politics: The Geographical Mediation of State and Society*. Abingdon: Routledge. https://doi.org/10.4324/9781315756585.

Aldana Reyes, Xavier. 2020. 'A Gothic Barcelona? Carlos Ruiz Zafón's The Cemetery of Forgotten Books Series and Franco's Legacy'. In *The New Urban Gothic: Global Gothic in the Age of the Anthropocene*, eds. Holly-Gale Millette and Ruth Heholt, pp. 237–50. Palgrave Gothic. Cham: Springer International Publishing. https://doi.org/10.1007/978-3-030-43777-0_14.

Anderson, Jon Lee. 2013. 'Private Eyes: A Crime Novelist Navigates Cuba's Shifting Reality'. *New Yorker*, 13 October. www.newyorker.com/magazine/2013/10/21/private-eyes.

Aykol, Esmahan. 2011. *Hotel Bosphorus (Kitapçı Dükkânı)*. Translated by Ruth Whitehouse. Kindle. Kati Hirschel Istanbul Mystery. London: Bitter Lemon Press.

Baker, Ray Stannard. 1922. *Adventures in Contentment*. New York: Doubleday, Page & Co.

Baxter, Valerie. 1956. *Shirley: Young Bookseller*. Bodley Head Career Book for Girls. London: Bodley Head.

Bennett, Arnold. 1923. *Riceyman Steps*. London: Cassell & Co.

Bivald, Katarina. 2013. *The Readers of Broken Wheel Recommend (Läsarna i Broken Wheel Rekommenderar)*. Translated by Alice Menzies. London: Vintage.

Block, Lawrence. 1977. *Burglars Can't Be Choosers*. Burglar 1. New York: Random House.

Brownfield, Elizabeth. 2020. 'Is This Bookstore That Inspired Harry Potter the Most Beautiful in the World?' *Forbes*, 30 March. www.forbes.com/sites/elizabethbrownfield/2020/03/30/is-this-book

store-thought-to-have-inspired-harry-potter-the-most-beautiful-in-the-world/.

Bruhm, Steven. 2002. 'The Contemporary Gothic: Why We Need It'. In *Cambridge Companion to Gothic Fiction*, ed. Jerrold E. Hogle, pp. 259–76. Cambridge Companions to Literature. Cambridge: Cambridge University Press. https://doi.org/10.1017/CCOL05217912 43.013.

Buzbee, Lewis. 2008. *Yellow-Lighted Bookshop (a Memoir, a History)*. Minneapolis, MN: Graywolf Press.

Byron, Glennis. 2012. 'Gothic, Grabbit and Run: Carlos Ruiz Zafón and the Gothic Marketplace'. In *The Gothic in Contemporary Literature and Popular Culture*, eds. J. Edwards and A. S. Monnet. Abingdon: Routledge.

Cacek, P. D. 2002. 'A Book By Its Cover'. In *Shelf Life: Fantastic Stories Celebrating Bookstores*, ed. Greg Ketter, pp. 195–210. Minneapolis, MN: Dreamhaven Books.

Casey, Edward S. 1996. 'How to Get from Space to Place in a Fairly Short Stretch of Time: Phenomenological Prolegomena'. In *Senses of Place*, eds. Steven Feld and Keith H. Basso, 1st ed., pp. 13–52. School of American Research Advanced Seminar Series. Santa Fe, NM: School of American Research Press.

Chatterjee, Paroma. 2020. 'A Tale of Two Bookshops: Sex and Books and The Big Sleep'. *Bright Lights Film Journal*, 15 June. https://brightslightsfilm.com/celebrating-world-book-day-tale-two-bookshops-sex-books-big-sleep/.

Chernofsky, Jacob L. 1986. 'Biblo and Tannen: A Fourth Avenue Landmark'. *BA Bookmans Weekly*, 14 April, 1666–71.

Colgan, Jenny. 2016. *The Bookshop on the Corner*. London: HarperCollins.

Cossé, Laurence. 2012. *A Novel Bookstore (Au Bon Roman)*. Translated by Alison Anderson. London: Europa Editions.

Cresswell, Tim. 2009. 'Place'. In *International Encyclopaedia of Human Geography*, eds. Rob Kitchin and Nigel Thrift, pp. 169–77. Oxford: Elsevier. https://doi.org/10.1016/B978-008044910-4.00310-2.

Daly, Steven and Nathaniel Wice. 1995. *Alt.Culture: An A-Z Guide to 90s America*. New York: Fourth Estate.

Darling, Will Y. 1931. *The Private Papers of a Bankrupt Bookseller*. Edinburgh: Oliver & Boyd.

Davis, Madeleine. 2005. 'Is Spain Recovering Its Memory? Breaking the "Pacto Del Olvido"'. *Human Rights Quarterly* 27 (3): 858–80. https://doi.org/10.1353/hrq.2005.0034.

De Angelis, Augusto and Joshua Sinclair. 1936. *Death in a Bookstore (Sei Donne e Un Libro)*. Milan: Edizioni Minerva.

De Certeau, Michel. 1984. *The Practice of Everyday Life*. Berkeley: University of California Press.

Dickens, Charles. 1993. *Oliver Twist*, ed. Fred Kaplan. Norton Critical ed. New York: W. W. Norton.

Duffy, Carol Ann. 2016. *Off the Shelf: A Celebration of Bookshops in Verse*. London: Pan Macmillan.

Dunning, John. 1992. *Booked to Die*. Kindle. Cliff Janeway Novel 1. New York: Simon & Schuster.

Dunton, John. 1818. *The Life and Errors of John Dunton, Citizen of London: With the Lives and Characters of More Than a Thousand Contemporary Divines*. Vol. 1. 2 vols. London: J. Nichols & Bentley.

Fitzgerald, Penelope. 1978. *The Bookshop*. London: Gerald Duckworth & Company.

Frost, Robert. 1947. *A Masque of Mercy*. New York: Henry Holt & Company.

George, Nina. 2015. *The Little Paris Bookshop*. London: Hachette.

Hand, Elizabeth. 2010. 'Laurence Cossé's "A Novel Bookstore"'. *Washington Post*, 6 November, sec. Book World. www.washingtonpost.com/wp-dyn/content/article/2010/11/05/AR2010110506764.html.

Hart, Carolyn G. 1987. *Death on Demand*. Death on Demand 1. New York: Bantam Crimeline.

2005. 'A Single Step'. *Mystery Readers Journal: Journal of Mystery Readers International* 21 (3): 43–4.

Harvey, David. 1990. *The Condition of Postmodernity: An Enquiry into the Origins of Cultural Change*. Oxford: Blackwell.

Hawks, Howard. 1946. *The Big Sleep*. Crime, Film-Noir, Mystery. www.imdb.com/title/tt0038355/.

Hay, Sheridan. 2010. *The Secret of Lost Things*. London: Harper Collins.

Henshaw, Sarah. 2014a. 'Living by the Book: The Floating Bookshop's Chapter of Accidents'. *The Independent*, 1 April. www.independent.co.uk/arts-entertainment/books/features/living-book-floating-bookshop-9226778.html.

2014b. *The Bookshop That Floated Away*. London: Hachette.

Highland, Kristin D. In Press. *The Spaces of Bookselling: Stores, Streets, and Pages*. Cambridge: Cambridge University Press.

Hillman, Robert. 2018. *The Bookshop of the Broken Hearted*. New York: Faber & Faber.

Hoffman, Nina Kiriki. 2002. 'Escapes'. In *Shelf Life: Fantastic Stories Celebrating Bookstores*, ed. Greg Ketter, pp. 195–210. Minneapolis, MN: Dreamhaven Books.

Hund, Alycia M., Martin Schmettow and Matthijs L. Noordzij. 2012. 'The Impact of Culture and Recipient Perspective on Direction Giving in the Service of Wayfinding'. *Journal of Environmental Psychology* 32 (4): 327–36. https://doi.org/10.1016/j.jenvp.2012.05.007.

Hunicke, Robin, Marc LeBlanc and Robert Zubek. 2004. 'MDA: A Formal Approach to Game Design and Game Research'. In *Proceedings of the AAAI Workshop on Challenges in Game AI*, 04–04. www.aaai.org/Papers/Workshops/2004/WS-04-04/WS04-04-001.pdf.

James, P. D. 2013. 'Who Killed the Golden Age of Crime?' *The Spectator*, 14 December. www.spectator.co.uk/article/p-d-james-who-killed-the-golden-age-of-crime-.

Kamali, Marjan. 2019. *The Stationery Shop*. New York: Gallery Books.

Kelly, Seana. 2020. *The Slaughtered Lamb Bookstore and Bar*. Sam Quinn Series 1. New York: NYLA.

   2021. *Dead Don't Drink at Lafitte's, The*. Sam Quinn Series 2. New York: NYLA.

King, Burton L., Jane Grey, Willard Dashiell and Edward MacKay. 1916. *Man and His Angel*. Drama. Triumph Films (II).

Laing, Audrey and Jo Royle. 2013. 'Examining Chain Bookshops in the Context of "Third Place"'. *International Journal of Retail & Distribution Management* 41 (1): 27–44. https://doi.org/10/gfjwnh.

Lanyon, Josh. 2007a. *A Dangerous Thing*. 4th ed. Adrien English Mysteries 2. Albion, NY: MLR Press.

   2007b. *Fatal Shadows*. 4th ed. Adrien English Mysteries 1. Albion, NY: MLR Press.

   2007c. *The Hell You Say*. Adrien English Mysteries 3. Albion, NY: MLR Press.

   2008a. *The Dark Tide*. 2nd ed. Adrien English Mysteries 5. Albion, NY: MLR Press.

   2008b. *Death of a Pirate King*. Adrien English Mysteries 4. Albion, NY: MLR Press.

   2013. *Stranger Things Have Happened: An Adrien English Write Your Own Damn Story*.

   Adrien English Mysteries 6. Palmdale, CA: JustJoshin Publishing.

   2016. *So This Is Christmas*. Adrien English Mysteries, 5.5. Palmdale, CA: JustJoshin Publishing.

Liddle, Kathy. 2019. 'Distribution Matters: Feminist Bookstores as Cultural Interaction Spaces'. *Cultural Sociology* 13 (1): 57–75. https://doi.org/10.1177/1749975518774732.

Malpas, Jeff. 2018. *Place and Experience: A Philosophical Topography*. Abingdon: Routledge.

Mantena, Rama Sundari. 2012. *The Origins of Modern Historiography in India: Antiquarianism and Philology, 1780–1880*. Cham: Springer International Publishing.

Massey, Doreen. 2005. *For Space*. London: SAGE.

    2012. 'Power-Geometry and a Progressive Sense of Place'. In *Mapping the Futures: Local Cultures, Gobal Change*, eds. Jon Bird, Barry Curtis, Tim Putnam, George Robertson and Lisa Tickner, pp. 59–69. Abingdon: Routledge. https://doi.org/10.4324/9780203977781-12.

Mearson, L. 1924. *The Whisper on the Stair*. New York: Macaulay.

Meddick, Judith. 2010. 'The Telling of Memory in *La Sombra Del Viento* by Carlos Ruiz Zafón'. *Romance Studies* 28 (4): 246–58. https://doi.org/10.1179/174581510X12817121842092.

Meyler, Deborah. 2013. *The Bookstore*. New York: Simon & Schuster.

Miller, Agnes. 1928. The Colfax Book-Plate. *Midvale Journal Sentinel*, 11.

Miller, Laura J. 2006. *Reluctant Capitalists: Bookselling and the Culture of Consumption*. Chicago: University of Chicago Press.

Milton, John. (1644). *Areopagitica*. https://milton.host.dartmouth.edu/reading_room/areopagitica/text.html

Mondlin, Marvin and Roy Meador. 2005. *Book Row: An Anecdotal and Pictorial History of the Antiquarian Book Trade*. New York: Carroll & Graf Publishers.

Morley, Christopher. 1917. *Parnassus on Wheels*. New York: Random House.

    1923. *The Haunted Bookshop*. Bookshop Edition. Garden City, NY: Doubleday, Doran & Co.

    1955. *Parnassus on Wheels*. Philadelphia, PA: Lippincott.

Oldenburg, Ray. 1989. *The Great Good Place: Cafes, Coffee Shops, Bookstores, Bars, Hair Salons, and Other Hangouts at the Heart of a Community*. Philadelphia, PA: Da Capo Press.

Oldenburg, Ray and Dennis Brissett. 1982. 'The Third Place'. *Qualitative Sociology* 5 (4): 265–84. https://doi.org/10.1007/BF00986754.

Orwell, George. 1936. *Keep the Aspidistra Flying*. London: Victor Gollancz.

Osborne, Huw Edwin, ed. 2015. *Rise of the Modernist Bookshop*. Farnham, UK: Ashgate.

Padura, Leonardo. 2003. *Havana Fever (La Neblina Del Ayer)*. Translated by Peter Bush. London: Bitter Lemon Press.

    2021. *The Transparency of Time (La Transparencia Del Tiempo)*. Translated by Anna Kushner. Mario Condo 9. London: Bitter Lemon Press.

Oxford English Dictionary. 2021. 'Bookshop, n.' In *OED Online*. Oxford: Oxford University Press. www.oed.com/view/Entry/356943#eid2786 01607.

Page, Marco. 1938. *Fast Company*. New York: Dodd Mead.

Parker, J. (2012). 'Conceptions of Place, Space and Narrative: Past, Present and Future'. *Amsterdam International Electronic Journal for Cultural Narratology*, 7, 74–101.

Passini, Romedi. 1996. 'Wayfinding Design: Logic, Application and Some Thoughts on Universality'. *Design Studies* 17 (3): 319–31. https://doi.org/10.1016/0142-694X(96)00001-4.

Richmond Ellis, Robert. 2006. 'Reading the Spanish Past: Library Fantasies in Carlos Ruiz Zafón's *La Sombra Del Viento*'. *Bulletin of Spanish Studies* 83 (6): 839–54. https://doi.org/10.1080/14753820600863907.

Riley, John D. 2004. *Else Fine . . . : Little Tales of Horror from Libraries and Bookshops*. Northampton, MA: Benjamin Press.

Roberts, William. 1895. *The Book-Hunter in London: Historical and Other Studies of Collectors and Collecting*. London: Elliot Stock. www.guten berg.org/ebooks/22607.

Sebastian, Pradeep. 2017. *The Book Hunters of Katpadi: A Bibliomystery*. London: Hachette.

Shay, Frank. 1924. 'Bookselling on the Broad Highroad; Confessions of Frank Shay Agent His "Peregrinating Palanquin of Bibliopolic Treasures"'. *New York Times Book Review*, 11 May.

Sicart, Miguel. 2008. 'Defining Game Mechanics'. *Game Studies* 8 (2). Milton, J. (1644). *Areopagitica*. https://milton.host.dartmouth.edu/reading_room/areopagitica/text.html
http://gamestudies.org/0802/articles/sicart?viewType=Print&viewClass=Print.

Simine, Silke Arnold-de. 2013. 'Memory Boom, Memory Wars and Memory Crises'. In *Mediating Memory in the Museum: Trauma, Empathy, Nostalgia*, ed. Silke Arnold-de Simine, pp. 14–19. Palgrave Macmillan Memory Studies. London: Palgrave Macmillan. https://doi.org/10.1057/9781137352644_3.

Slater, John Herbert. 1898. *The Romance of Book-Collecting*. Boston, MA: Frances P. Harper. www.gutenberg.org/ebooks/46237.

Sloan, Robin. 2012. *Mr Penumbra's 24-Hour Bookstore*. London: Atlantic Books Ltd.

Smith, Gibbs M. 2009. *The Art of the Bookstore*. Layton, UT: Gibbs Smith.

Stableford, Brian. 2001. 'The Haunted Bookshop'. In *Dark Terrors 5: The Gollancz Book of Horror*, eds. Stephen Jones and David Sutton, pp. 331–53. London: Gollancz.

Stephens, Andrew. 2012. 'Interview: Carlos Ruiz Zafón'. *Sydney Morning Herald*, 23 June. www.smh.com.au/entertainment/books/interview-carlos-ruiz-zafon-20120621-20p0w.html.

Sullivan, Matthew. 2017. *Midnight at the Bright Ideas Bookstore*. New York: Simon & Schuster.

Teicher, Oren. 2012. 'The CEO Report from ABA's 2012 Annual Membership Meeting'. www.bookweb.org/news/ceo-report-aba%E2%80%99s-2012-annual-membership-meeting.

TimesMachine. 1911. 'Gutenberg Bible Sold for $50,000'. *New York Times*, 25 April.

Trotman, Tiffany Gagliardi. 2007. 'Haunted Noir: Neo-Gothic Barcelona in Carlos Ruiz Zafón's La Sombra Del Viento'. *Romance Studies* 25 (4): 269–77. https://doi.org/10.1179/174581507x235598.

Tuan, Yi-fu. 1977. *Space and Place: The Perspective of Experience*. London: University of Minnesota Press.

Walk, Wolfgang, Daniel Görlich and Mark Barrett. 2017. 'Design, Dynamics, Experience (DDE): An Advancement of the MDA Framework for Game Design'. In *Game Dynamics: Best Practices in Procedural and Dynamic Game Content Generation*, eds. Oliver Korn and Newton Lee, pp. 27–45. Cham: Springer International Publishing. https://doi.org/10.1007/978-3-319-53088-8_3.

Wells, Carolyn. 1936. *Murder in the Bookshop*. Kindle. London: Collins Crime Club. https://gutenberg.net.au/ebooks19/1900751h.html.

Wells, Carolyn and Alfred F. Goldsmith. 1922. *A Concise Bibliography of the Works of Walt Whitman with a Supplement*. Cambridge, MA: Houghton-Mifflin.

Wiseman, Beth. 2022. *The Bookseller's Promise*. Amish Bookstore. Grand Rapids, Michigan: Zondervan Books.

Zafón, Carlos Ruiz. 2001. *The Shadow of the Wind (La Sombra Del Viento)*. Translated by Lucia Graves. Cemetery of Forgotten Books 1. London: Weidenfeld & Nicolson.

Zevin, Gabrielle. 2014. *The Collected Works of A.J. Fikry [The Storied Life of A.J. Fikry]*. London: Little Brown.

Dedicated to Ben and Ruth Muse and the Parnassus Book Service they created.

Cambridge Elements ≡

Publishing and Book Culture

SERIES EDITOR
Samantha Rayner
University College London

Samantha Rayner is Professor of Publishing and Book Cultures at UCL. She is also Director of UCL's Centre for Publishing, Co-Director of the Bloomsbury CHAPTER (Communication History, Authorship, Publishing, Textual Editing and Reading) and Co-Chair of the Bookselling Research Network.

ASSOCIATE EDITOR
Leah Tether
University of Bristol

Leah Tether is Professor of Medieval Literature and Publishing at the University of Bristol. With an academic background in medieval French and English literature and a professional background in trade publishing, Leah has combined her expertise and developed an international research profile in book and publishing history from manuscript to digital.

About the Series

This series aims to fill the demand for easily accessible, quality texts available for teaching and research in the diverse and dynamic fields of Publishing and Book Culture. Rigorously researched and peer-reviewed Elements will be published under themes, or 'Gatherings'. These Elements should be the first check point for researchers or students working on that area of publishing and book trade history and practice: we hope that, situated so logically at Cambridge University Press, where academic publishing in the UK began, it will develop to create an unrivalled space where these histories and practices can be investigated and preserved.

Cambridge Elements $^{\equiv}$

Publishing and Book Culture

Bookshops and Bookselling

Gathering Editor: Eben Muse

Eben Muse is Senior Lecturer in Digital Media at Bangor University and Co-Director of the Stephen Colclough Centre for the History and Culture of the Book. He studies the impact of digital technologies on the cultural and commercial space of bookselling, and he is part-owner of a used bookstore in the United States.

A full series listing is available at: www.cambridge.org/EPBC

Printed in the United States
by Baker & Taylor Publisher Services